DATE DUE

~~JAN 3 1 2001~~	APR 2 2 2011
~~JUN 2 8 2001~~	
~~APR 0 2 2003~~	
~~APR 3 0 2003~~	
~~FEB 2 4 2009~~	

HOW TO DISAGREE
WITHOUT BEING
DISAGREEABLE

Other Books by Suzette Haden Elgin

NONFICTION

Genderspeak: Men, Women, and the Gentle Art of Verbal Self-Defense
The Gentle Art of Verbal Self-Defense
More on the Gentle Art of Verbal Self-Defense
The Last Word on the Gentle Art of Verbal Self-Defense
Success with the Gentle Art of Verbal Self-Defense
Staying Well with the Gentle Art of Verbal Self-Defense
The Gentle Art of Written Self-Defense
You Can't *Say* That to Me!
BusinessSpeak: Using the Gentle Art of Persuasion
to Get What You Want at Work
The Gentle Art of Communicating With Kids
Try to Feel It *My* Way: New Help for Touch Dominant People
and Those Who Care About Them

TEXTBOOKS

Guide to Transformational Grammar (with John Grinder, Ph.D.)
Pouring Down Words
What is Linguistics?

NOVELS

The Communipaths
Furthest
At the Seventh Level
Twelve Fair Kingdoms
The Grand Jubilee
And Then There'll Be Fireworks
Star-Anchored, Star-Angered
Native Tongue
Yonder Comes the Other End of Time
Native Tongue II: The Judas Rose
Native Tongue III: Earthsong

Audio Programs by Suzette Haden Elgin

Mastering the Gentle Art of Verbal Self-Defense
Success with the Gentle Art of Verbal Self-Defense
The Gentle Art of Verbal Self-Defense for Parents and Kids
(with Rebecca Haden, M.A.)
The Gentle Art of Verbal Self-Defense for Parents and Teenagers
(with Rebecca Haden, M.A.)

HOW TO DISAGREE WITHOUT BEING DISAGREEABLE

Getting Your Point Across with the Gentle Art of Verbal Self-Defense

Suzette Haden Elgin, Ph.D.

John Wiley & Sons, Inc.

New York · Chichester · Weinheim · Brisbane · Singapore · Toronto

Library of Congress Cataloging-in-Publication Data

Elgin, Suzette Haden.
    How to disagree without being disagreeable : getting your point across with the gentle art of verbal self-defense / Suzette Haden Elgin.
        p.   cm.
    Includes bibliographical references and index.
    ISBN 0-471-15701-5 (cloth : alk. paper). — ISBN 0-471-15705-8 (pbk. : alk. paper)
        1. Verbal self-defense.   2. Interpersonal conflict.
    3. Interpersonal communication.   I. Title.
    BF637.V47E4314   1997
    153.6—dc20   96-35430

Printed in the United States of America

10 9 8 7 6 5 4 3 2

CONTENTS

ACKNOWLEDGMENTS

This is the twelfth book in the *Gentle Art of Verbal Self-Defense* series; as with the others, I am deeply indebted to the many scholars whose work laid the foundations on which mine is based. I am especially grateful to the thousands of people who have spoken or written to me about their questions and comments and personal experiences; their input has been invaluable to me. Special thanks go to Leonard Newmark of UCSD, who taught me how to make people want to learn and how to bring them through the learning process successfully, and to my editors—PJ Dempsey, Chris Jackson, and Joanne Palmer—at John Wiley & Sons. My long-suffering family has my thanks as always, for the support and tolerance provided. The responsibility for mistakes and omissions is of course entirely mine.

If you have any comments or questions, please feel free to contact me directly; I will get back to you as quickly as I can.

Suzette Haden Elgin, Ph.D.
PO Box 1137, Huntsville AR 72740-1137
Email: ocls@ipa.net

ABOUT THE AUTHOR

Suzette Haden Elgin has a doctorate in linguistics from the University of California San Diego, and is Associate Professor Emeritus (retired) from San Diego State University's Department of Linguistics. She is an applied psycholinguist, and the founder of the Ozark Center for Language Studies, which she directs from her home near Huntsville, Arkansas. She is the author of the *Gentle Art of Verbal Self-Defense* series (the first book of which has now sold more than one million copies), as well as numerous audio programs, textbooks and novels; she writes and publishes two newsletters (*Linguistics & Science Fiction* and the *Touch Dominance Quarterly*); she maintains a heavy schedule of seminars all around the United States and a private consulting practice. She has five children and nine grandchildren. She can be reached for information about seminars, consulting, or other services at OCLS, PO Box 1137, Huntsville AR 72740-1137, or by email at ocls@ipa.net.

HOW TO DISAGREE
WITHOUT BEING
DISAGREEABLE

INTRODUCTION

On April 19, 1995, with the bombing of the federal building in Oklahoma City, the United States changed forever. Not because we had not had disasters and terrorist attacks before, but because this one was *different*.

This time the target was an office building in America's heartland, in a sleepy city that everyone thought of as a safe place to live. This time many of the victims were tiny children and babies. The destructive force wasn't a monstrous storm or an attack by an enemy nation; it was said to be one of our own people, someone just like us, just like the people next door. And this time, because of our sophisticated media, the whole tragedy took place in *real* time, right before our eyes and our ears. Nothing like this had happened to us since the Civil War (the most *un*civil of our wars), in a time when reports on the terror and suffering could take weeks to arrive.

In the aftermath of the Oklahoma City bombing, many people—including the President of the United States—were heard suggesting publicly that some of the blame for what had happened should be assigned to our society's violent *language*. This also was new. We are accustomed to thinking of language as "only talk," after all. We are a people fiercely devoted to the protection of freedom of speech, and rightly so. Nevertheless, the President and the experts came forward in the spring of 1995 to suggest that there are limits, that hate speech was at least indirectly responsible for what had happened, and to ask for a return to "civil discourse" in America.

Bill Clinton told us solemnly that people who use such language "leave the impression, by their very words, that violence is acceptable" (Alter, 1995). Michael Kramer wrote that "everyone is obliged to demand a more honest and a more civil discourse," and suggested that the very phrase "civil discourse" has now become a contradiction in terms (Kramer, 1995). Deborah Prothrow-Stith wrote that "being mean is popular. In fact, the skills for getting along—negotiation, empathy, forgiveness—are those usually ascribed to wimps" and called for immediate efforts to bring about change ("The Power of Nonviolence," *Best of Technology Review*, Spring 1995).

To those of us who have been struggling for decades to convince others that language is not "just talk" but a powerful force we must learn to use more carefully, these statements were very welcome. The debate that followed as talk show hosts, tabloid journalists, politicians, and special interest groups came roaring out of the chutes to protest their innocence was also welcome. Amazing as it was to hear rational adults declaring that there is no connection between physical violence in America and the current flood of violent American speech, at least there was a debate on the issue instead of indifference. But it didn't last long, not even when the assassination of Israeli Prime Minister Yitzhak Rabin brought on yet another round of public figures suggesting a link between hateful words and murder.

The horror of Oklahoma City is burned into our memories so deeply that we will never forget it. But it's now part of the past, and Rabin's death happened far away. The debate has faded. If the proposed threat to our safety had been chemicals or bacteria in our air or water, I believe we would have reacted very differently, but the alleged threat was language. "Only" language.

The *question* was certainly clear to all of us: "*Does violent language lead to violent acts?*" But we didn't demand that scholars and scientists and experts investigate until they could give us a solid answer that would serve as a basis for future behavior. We've let the issue go back to being the concern of a handful of pundits and academics and think tanks; we have put it out of our minds. We have focused instead on increasing security procedures in our airports and public places, on putting more police on the streets, on building more prisons, on producing better bulletproof vests—in short, on providing everything a society requires for dealing with *physical* violence. The problem of *verbal* violence has once more been shoved to the back attic of our public attention.

This ought to surprise us. Logically, whether violence in language leads to violent acts is something that we *must* know, and as quickly as possible. Suppose the answer is yes. Then we should begin making substantial changes in many areas of our lives. If the answer is yes, we have to become responsible for the way we use our language, in exactly the same fashion that we hold ourselves responsible for the way we use our cars. If the answer is no, on the other hand, if no significant link exists between violent speech and violent acts, we can relax and go on as we are. Logically, we should be determined to know which of those answers is correct. Why *don't* we insist on knowing?

Frankly, I think it's because we already *do* know, from our own experience and our common sense. But we don't want our knowledge to be made conscious and brought out into the open where it can't be ignored. We're like the student in one of my linguistics classes who stood up at the end of the first week saying, "I do not choose to know these things—I can't afford to know them!" and walked out for good. We have let the public debate fade away because we are deeply afraid to acknowledge what we know.

As long as we hide our heads in the sand like this, we don't feel threatened. We don't have to make changes; we don't have to face the possibility that we ourselves (rather than some faceless "they" out there somewhere) create conditions that make the epidemic of violence in our homes and schools and workplaces and streets possible.

This reaction is wholly natural and understandable. Nobody wants to look at the media's pictures of victims of bombings and knifings and shootings and think, "I had something to do with that." Nevertheless, in spite of our natural reluctance, the time has come when we have to demand the answers to some hard questions about language and violence. The purpose of this book is to let us begin exploring those questions together, as rational adults. For example . . .

Does it make sense to say that pain caused by fists and guns is wrong, but it's okay to cause pain with words—as do the stars on talk shows and situation comedies, earning our laughter and applause?

Does it make sense to support and admire talk shows composed almost entirely of vicious and hurtful talk and then claim to be astonished when our young people go out and hurt one another physically?

Is it true (as some military experts claimed after the Tailhook disgrace) that unless you tolerate ugly language you can't produce top fighter pilots and winning football teams?

Can we say with reasonable assurance that although hate speech might lead to an occasional fist fight, it has nothing to do with major physical violence and it's silly to worry about it? Or are violent words practice for the "real thing," a sort of training wheels for physical violence?

We need to know; it's time for us to settle this. If the idea of a link between hateful language and hateful acts is nothing but a neurotic fantasy, we need to know that so that we'll waste no more time or resources on the concept. If the link is real, however, it's equally urgent for us to know *that*, so that we can decide what (if anything) we can and should do about it. We don't need to foist this off on some "blue ribbon panel of experts," either. Not this time. Because where our language is concerned, we—the community of people who speak it—*are* the experts.

We can begin by staking out our territory and defining our terms: What is the language we propose to investigate—the language so often referred to as "hate speech"—and how do we recognize it?

WHAT IS "HATE SPEECH"?

Few of us, asked simply "Do you approve of hate speech?", would say that we do, even if we are strong defenders of our right to use it when we choose to. But what is it, exactly? There are examples that are very clear:

- KFYI (Phoenix) talk show host Bob Mohan stated on the air that gun control advocate Sarah Brady "ought to be put down. A humane shot at a veterinarian's would be an easy way to do it." (*Minneapolis Star-Tribune*, February 24, 1995.)

- In San Francisco various talk show hosts encouraged their listeners to shoot illegal immigrants for reward money. (*Minneapolis Star-Tribune*, February 24, 1995.)

- We all heard or read about the tapes in which LAPD detective Mark Fuhrman stated that all gang members and dope dealers should be rounded up and shot. (Reibstein, 1995.)

Almost everyone will agree that, whether we approve of it or not, these examples are hate speech. But these are the rare and extreme cases, out at the lunatic fringe. Most of the time, it's not so simple.

Suppose I'm out walking, minding my own business, and a stranger leans out the window of a nearby building and yells at me, "HEY, YOU! You stupid hillbilly BROAD! Go on back to the HILLS, where you beLONG!" What if, instead of yelling about my origins, the stranger uses his most lustful bellow to describe in detail the sexual acts he would like me to join him in? Is that hate speech?

Suppose I'm at work and my supervisor comes over to my desk and says, "None of the letters you did yesterday were done correctly—but that's all right, dear. After all, everybody knows you're not qualified for this job; I'm sure you did the very best you could." Or suppose that instead of "you're" not qualified she says that "you people" aren't qualified. Are her remarks hate speech?

What if a Republican on my bus starts calling Democrats ugly names in front of me and my kids, and I say, "I'm a Democrat, and I resent the things you're saying—especially in front of my children! At LEAST the Democrats haven't lost their MINDS like you RePUBlicans have!" What if the speaker who offends me is not a stranger but a friend? Are either or both of us using hate speech? What if a teenager, told that she absolutely may *not* go to an unchaperoned slumber party, shouts, "I HATE you!" Is *that* hate speech?

This isn't a simple matter. People disagree about what constitutes offensive language. I'm a southerner from the Ozark mountains. Many people who would unhesitatingly call it hate speech if they heard someone say "nigger" or "kike" are quick to say, "Hey, lighten up!" when I object to being called "hillbilly" or to hearing one of my male relatives referred to as a "Bubba." One person's unforgivable insult is quite often what somebody else claims as "just kidding around."

Although the language I've described is surely *hate*ful, such talk often has nothing to do with hate. Notice that the single example where someone actually declares hatred, the language of the angry teenager, is the one *least* likely to be labeled "hate speech." If people used such language only when they were truly motivated by hatred the term might be useful, but they don't. Far more often, ugly talk is due to ignorance, or fear, or anger (not necessarily anger connected to what's being said). Often it's due to exhaustion, or a host of other problems, including greed or a desire to show off. We're frantic, we're frustrated, we're tired, we're confused, we have bills to pay—in short, we're human—and so we speak *hatefully*. But hate is not what it's about. "Uncivil discourse" isn't strong enough to cover shouted ethnic slurs and obscenities. "Verbal abuse," "psychological abuse," and "emotional abuse," are used to refer to ugly language, as is "verbal violence," but the heavy semantic weight of the Abuser/Victim concept frequently makes them a poor fit, and neither psychological nor emotional abuse is restricted entirely to language.

We need a term that's easily understood, that comes from the vocabulary of ordinary people, and that is neutral enough to apply to the very broad range of language involved. I suggest *hostile language* as our cover term. We can accurately apply it to any of the examples above, including the teenager's "I HATE you!" And saying "language" rather than "speech" makes it clear that we're including *nonverbal* communication—tone of voice, gesture, facial expression, and so on—as well as words.

HOW DO WE RECOGNIZE HOSTILE LANGUAGE?

The question of how we recognize hostile language when we encounter it only seems difficult because of a common misunderstanding about our language: the idea that what matters is the *words* we say. For English, that's simply false. What matters, more than 90 percent of the time, is not our words but the body language that goes with them, and especially the tune the words are set to. There are no inherently hostile *words*.

I can take the most repulsive label, the most gross descriptive phrase, the ugliest name, and *say it to you with so much tenderness that all its negative characteristics are cancelled*. I can tell you that you are "a disgusting vicious contemptible monster." I can even throw in a sexist or racist epithet to top it off. And I can say *all* of that in such a way that you will feel only complimented. Political correctness may make you feel obligated to ask me to revise some part of what I said, but you will know absolutely that I was expressing only positive emotions toward you when I spoke.

Because written language doesn't let us hear the tune along with the words, it's hard to know whether it's hostile or not. I would never be safe *writing* to you with the sort of words I just described; I had to be extremely careful even in my description. But few of us have to worry about hateful mail; the problem is hateful *speech*. And when we hear words spoken we have little or no difficulty recognizing hostile language, even when the person talking tries to deny it. That is the source of the very accurate critical comment, "It wasn't what you said, it was the way you said it!" "The way you say it"—the melody behind the words, with its pitches and rhythms and subtle shadings of intonation—is in fact what almost always matters for English.

Hostile English has two primary characteristics:

1. It relies heavily on very personal vocabulary—"I, you, this company, this family, this department, this job," and on proper names.

2. It contains acoustic stresses—*emphasis*—on words and parts of words, stresses that aren't needed for any purpose except to express hostility.

   If I say to you, "We didn't leave on the third, we left on the <u>fifth</u>," you know that the extra emphasis on "fifth" is necessary to contrast "fifth" with "third." If I say, "<u>Hey</u>, I <u>won</u> the SWEEP-stakes!," you know that I need the emphasis on "hey, won, sweep" to carry the message that I am tremendously excited about my announcement. But when I say, "You could at least TRY to get to work on TIME once in a while!," you know that the emphasis on "try" and "time" has no purpose except to express hostility. You can trust your internal grammar to make such judgments for you, *as long as you are paying attention, so that you hear the tunes accurately.*

Sometimes the first characteristic is missing from what's said because the speaker is relying on the situation to carry it, as in "People who never get to WORK on time shouldn't exPECT to keep their JOBS!" Even so, when we keep hearing emphasis that isn't needed for other grammatical reasons, we reliably recognize the language as hostile. When both characteristics are there in a sequence of language at the same time, there's no question in our minds—it's hostile.

Just one thing needs to be added, so that no confusion creeps in here. The characteristics listed identify hostile language very well. They do *not* identify language as libelous, or obscene, or slanderous, or defamatory, or any of the other categories used in lawsuits. They don't identify it in critical terms, as appropriate or inappropriate, foolish or wise, intelligent or stupid, elegant or clumsy. Those are separate issues.

FOUR QUESTIONS TO ANSWER

In this book we will take a good long look at hostile language and seek answers for these four questions:

1. Is hostile language *bad*?

Isn't it "just talk"? After all, it's not guns or cyanide; it's only words, right? Maybe. The U.S. Catholic Conference of Bishops wrote in 1992 that "violence in any form—physical, sexual, psychological, or verbal—is sinful." Sinful? Should the bishops lighten up?

2. Is hostile language *necessary*?

Even if we disapprove of hostile language, perhaps we just have to accept it. Maybe it's like taxes, an unpleasant but unavoidable part of life in an imperfect world. We do have to give others messages that aren't all sweetness and light. We do have to discipline our children, and offer constructive criticism to employees and students and colleagues. We do have to do performance reviews and evaluations; we do have to stand up for ourselves and for our beliefs. It may be that we *need* hostile language and can't get through our days without it, regardless of how undesirable it is.

3. Why do we use hostile language? For what reasons and purposes? Why are we so *fond* of it?

Many people have told me that they believe hostile language is used as a weapon to cause pain and distress, but that they have to use it because otherwise people will take advantage and walk all over them. They say, *"Everybody's out to get you; you have to get them before they get you. That's just the way things are."* Others have told me that hostile language is a kind of sport, like tennis—just a game they enjoy playing. Law enforcement officers, for example, have told me in training sessions that if they had to give up hostile talk it would take all the fun out of their job. They say, *"I like to get people going; I get a kick out of it!"* There are also those who assure me that human beings are by nature brutes, that aggressiveness and hostility are part of the definition of a human being. They say, *"You can no more get rid of hostile talk than you can get rid of wars."* Are they right? Certainly it's true that the quickest way for a talk show host or a television sitcom to develop high ratings is to showcase the meanest mouths in town.

4. What are the *alternatives* to hostile language? What can we use in its place?

Obviously, even if we all agree that hostile language is bad, if no other language is available to us for transmitting necessary negative messages, we're stuck with it. We need to find out if there are alternatives.

I'm going to propose a set of answers to these questions. I'm going to explain why hostile language is bad—dangerous, destructive, and morally wrong. I'm going to show that it's unnecessary, because although we do have to deliver messages with negative content, there is always a nonhostile way to construct them.

We have good reason to be hopeful. We got into this mess slowly, over a long period of time, and we've come to believe that it's "just the way things are" only because it's now such a familiar part of our daily lives. I don't believe human beings are "born to argue"; I think it's mostly habit. The reason many of us are so genuinely *reluctant* to give up our hostile language is that it's become a dearly beloved plague; we've just grown used to it. Getting hostile language out of our lives, far from being an activity suitable only for saints and wimps, is the smartest investment we can make in our own well-being.

ABOUT THIS BOOK

This book has three parts. Part One (this introduction, and Chapters 1 and 2) provides an overview of the problem, with essential terms and concepts. It then moves on to our first two questions: Is hostile language bad? Is hostile language necessary?

Part Two (Chapters 3 through 5) lays the foundation that has to be constructed if we decide to eliminate hostile language from our speech. Chapter 3 answers our third question—Why do people use hostile language?—and provides the information we have to have to avoid responding to such language with an emotional reaction that feeds the hostility and makes matters worse. Chapter 4 explains why the skill of active listening is critical to our project, and how we can improve our listening skills. In Chapter 5 we examine the power of metaphors to shape our thoughts and behavior, and consider ways to replace the *ARGUMENT IS WAR* metaphor with one less likely to encourage violence.

Part Three (Chapters 6 through 10) presents a set of simple and practical alternatives to hostile language—patterns and skills that we can use to convey all our necessary negative messages without having to resort to hostile language.

There is a widespread impression today that gender plays a very large part in hostile language, and that there's something special about cross-gender communication that requires our attention. Whenever that issue is relevant, you will find sections specifically devoted to it, titled "He Said/She Said."

Throughout the book I will try to make an end run of sorts around the difficult task of setting down the tune of English in written words. When quoted speech is intended to show hostility I will use underlining to indicate extra emphasis, and all capital letters—as in "What's the MATTER with you, ANYway?"—to show even stronger emphasis. This is no substitute for actually hearing the tunes, but it's a start, and it will be helpful.

At the end of the book you'll find a detailed bibliography that will lead you to both the original sources I refer to and to many sources of additional information, plus an index to help you move around in the book easily and efficiently.

PART ONE

OVERVIEW

1

IS HOSTILE LANGUAGE
BAD?

We are surrounded by language, everywhere we go and in every-thing we do, just as surely as we are surrounded by air. Even when we are alone and in silence, we keep up a steady stream of in-ternal self-talk. Language isn't just sounds and symbols and shapes. It's not just an "artifact" like a chair or a spoon. It is a human envi-ronment, and it brings with it all the qualities—and all the problems and responsibilities—that go with that status.

PROTECTING THE LANGUAGE ENVIRONMENT

There was a time when people in the United States had little concern for the physical environment. We would keep our own front yards green, and go to considerable trouble to put trash where we didn't have to look at it from our own windows, but that was about it. I'm old enough to remember when the popular wisdom was that nature was so huge, so abundant, so limitless that it could take care of itself. We really believed in those days that we could take all we wanted, without worrying about putting anything back and without worrying about our methods. We were sure that there would always be more than enough of all the things that make life in this huge country good and support our claim that every single one of us is entitled to "the pursuit of happiness."

In the past half-century, however, we've learned that we were wrong. We can and do run out of things that are necessary to our lives; we can and do cause damage, often long-lasting and severe, to our physical environment. Today we realize with dismay that because we were so slow to discover our error it may now be too late to set things right.

We've hardly even begun to consider the need to look after the *language* environment; the whole idea is new. When we talk about what would make up such an environment we say exactly the kinds of things we used to say about the physical one. We used to say "It's only dirt"; and now we say "It's only talk." We used to say that people who worried about pesticides were alarmists and troublemakers; we express the same judgment today of people who worry about the effects of language. We used to say that if there really *was* a problem, we had all the time in the world to fix it. "Right now," we'd say, "we have more <u>important</u> things to worry about!"

It took us a long time to realize that we were ruining our physical environment, because most of us weren't in charge of some giant factory that was dumping tons of toxic waste into nearby rivers. We accepted the idea that people like *that* were doing harm, but we were convinced that what *we* did was okay. If we threw a cigarette butt out the car window as we drove along, what's one cigarette butt? So we sprayed our half dozen tomato plants with DDT, so what? What we did was on such a small scale—*it wasn't the same thing as what the factory owner did*. It took us decades to realize that when every individual insists on a personal right to pollute the environment on a very small scale, it adds up to pollution on an enormous scale.

Today, when we hear talk of a need to protect the language environment, we react the same way. We may agree that a talk show host who provides a daily diet of open insults about some group of people, and urges others to shoot them for bounty, could be dangerous. But we insist that what *we* do, our *own* hostile language, is harmless.

If we say to an employee or colleague, "What's the MATTER with you, can't you do ANYTHING RIGHT?", so what? As at least a dozen bosses have said to me, "They <u>work</u> for me; I pay their salaries. If they don't like the way I talk, that's <u>their</u> problem!" If we tell a child, "That's the stupidest thing I ever <u>heard</u> in my entire <u>life</u>, have you lost your MIND? Just keep QUIET about it and quit BOTHering me!", what's one sharp sentence or two to an annoying kid? If we say something that hurts a friend and then add, "Oh, I suppose NOW your FEELings are hurt! CAN'T you even take a JOKE?!," what difference does it make? *It's not the same thing as what the talk show host does—right?*

Obviously, we haven't yet realized that if every single one of us insists on his or her personal right to use just a *little* hostile language every day, the time will come when it reaches a critical mass and there's no room left for any other kind. Nor, as our young people grow more and more callous about violence, have we stopped to ask ourselves where they're going to find people using wholesome language, so that they can learn how that is done. It looks as though we haven't learned a thing. Why? We're not stupid, nor are we ignorant. Why haven't we learned?

THE TRAGEDY OF THE COMMONS

One reason for our indifference to the language environment is what is called "the tragedy of the commons." When pasture land is held in common, overgrazing always happens; when rivers and seas are held in common, overfishing is inevitable. As Matt Ridley and Bobbi S. Low wrote in the September 1993 *Atlantic Monthly*, "the benefits that each extra cow (or netful of fish) brings are reaped by its owner, but the costs of the extra strain it puts on the grass (or on fish stocks) are shared among all the users of what is held in common." People who need to put food on the family table by grazing a certain number of cows or catching a certain number of fish are unwilling (or sometimes unable) to focus their minds on what eventually might happen if everyone worries only about his or her *own* needs.

Similarly, people have discovered that they can put food on the table by ranting and raving on the radio or television, or by bullying their colleagues and employees. They've learned that they can gain confidence and self-esteem from using language to demonstrate their power over others, and that this not only makes them feel good but seems to help them get ahead. They've found that sarcasm is a quick

15

and easy way to make a child behave. They've found that ethnic jokes make people laugh, and it's pleasant to be a hit with the crowd. These are immediate and obvious rewards, the way bug-free tomatoes are; they have far more power to affect people than the alleged consequences of language behavior in some distant and hypothetical future.

Riddley and Low tell us that we have to find "individual incentives in favor of saving the atmosphere," or we will fail. Substitute "the language environment" for "the atmosphere" in that statement; it remains true. People do put benefits for themselves and their immediate families first. If they're aware that what they're doing poses a risk to their great-great-grandchildren, they assume that those descendants will figure out a way to deal with it. *We are not saints*. It's hassle enough planning for the coming few years, just getting from paycheck to paycheck, without trying to plan in terms of future generations. Unless we can find individual and personal incentives for keeping the language environment wholesome, with benefits that can clearly be seen to pay out in our own lifetimes, nobody will bother.

Fortunately, those incentives exist. But I find myself uneasily wondering whether the bombing in Oklahoma City is the linguistic equivalent of the destruction of the ozone layer—a sign that it may already be too late to do more than try to contain the damage and keep the situation from getting worse. I hope not. I think we still have time. But not *plenty* of time! We are right up against the limits, right now.

THE PHANTOM LANDFILL

Another reason we ignore the language environment is that the damage we do has no physical shape. Foul words and sentences have an advantage that used diapers and dead fish and spilled oil can never have: You can't *see* (or smell) them. If everyone in an area keeps throwing trash out into a ditch along the road, the time comes when that pile of waste is so obvious and ugly that it can't be ignored. At which point ordinary people, not just environmental extremists, object, and they keep on objecting until something is done.

Language, especially spoken language, isn't like that. No matter how enduring a memory people may have of hurtful things said to or about them, there never seems to be "anything there." The landfills for hostile language seem to be without limit—infinite linguistic space, free for the taking. Without a towering hill of smelly garbage to offend the eye and nose, or a horde of scavenging rats or buzzards to cause alarm, it's easy to conclude that civility is only for do-gooders and kooks.

THE BENEFITS OF ELIMINATING HOSTILE LANGUAGE

What we need is a clear and simple list of the immediate benefits of a wholesome language environment—benefits that are not phantoms but can be easily recognized in the real world that we all live in.

Here's the list.

First Benefit: More Safety and Security, at Less Cost

Suppose we set aside national tragedies such as the Oklahoma City bombing for the moment. They are rare, and—so far—they happen to only a few of us. Let's just look at the daily lives of ordinary people. Your own common sense and your experience in life will tell you that ordinary people past the age of three or four don't just walk up to others and start hitting; you don't need research studies to tell you that. First come angry words accompanied by angry facial expressions and gestures and tone of voice; first, there is an *argument*. Almost all physical violence, even between teenage street gangs, begins not with a drive-by shooting or a knife out of the darkness but with hostile *talk*.

If it went no farther than talk, that would be one thing, but it doesn't stop there. Here are some statistics—conservative ones taken from sober medical journals and government agency reports, not from tabloids—for you to consider. (All the statistics below refer to the United States, but the effects of violence are felt worldwide.) When there is disagreement about the numbers, I have selected the lowest figure. First there is hostile language, and then . . .

- There are one million premature deaths in the United States every year from homicide or suicide, and gunshot wounds are the leading cause of death for both white and African-American male teenagers. (Rosenberg, 1992)

- The United States is the most violent country in the industrialized world, with 2 million people beaten, knifed, shot or otherwise assaulted every year, 23,000 of them fatally. (Toufexis, 1993)

- More than 1.5 million women are battered by their male partners every year in the United States, with battering as the most common cause of female injury—more common than auto accidents, rapes, and muggings combined. (Arbeiter, 1991)

- In 1985 there were 8.7 million violent episodes between couples in the United States, of which 3.4 million could be described as severe—and the major risk factor for domestic violence between adults is that one of the adults has witnessed such episodes as a child, even if he or she was not directly involved. (Ammerman & Hersen, 1992)

- 30 percent of all women in the United States who arrive at an emergency department with injuries have been hurt by their male partners or ex-partners. (Chambliss, 1994)

You may be thinking that you don't live in an inner city, surrounded by violent physical crime; you don't beat your spouse and children and elderly parents or get in fistfights with your associates, and you don't know anybody who does. It may seem to you that although those statistics are shocking, they have nothing to do with you—they don't cost *you* anything. But I assure you—they *do*.

The statistics explain why insurance rates are so high. Look at the numbers again. One in every three women who arrives injured at an emergency room has suffered those injuries at the hands (or worse) of her male partner; battering is the most common source of injury for adult women today; violence is the leading cause of death in young men. . . . Who pays for all that? Who pays for the housing and care of the young children of all these injured people while they're being treated? The children (and elderly relatives) of the victims don't look after themselves: They are cared for out of your taxes and your charitable donations.

Those statistics are the reason we spend so much for "security." Property insurance against vandalism and arson and theft, for example. Guards to station inside public and private buildings. Law enforcement officers to patrol the streets. Courts in which to try people caught doing violence. Jails and prisons for locking up the violent, with still more guards. Tuition for private schools for our children, because no child can learn much in schoolrooms where the teacher has to devote most class time just to maintaining order. Extra gas and time spent in long commutes because living conveniently close to the workplace would put us and our families in personal danger. There are extra costs tacked on to every item we buy, including food, because the businesses that manufacture and store and sell those items have to have a way to cover the costs of *their* security.

The money that pays for all these things, even if we never suffer any violence directly, comes right out of our pockets. It's not other people who pay for it and it's not "the government." *We* are the ones who pay.

Verbal hostilities are the root of physical ones; most of the physical violence that is draining away our resources begins with "only talk." Therefore, learning to avoid hostile language (and to defuse it when we encounter it through no fault of our own) would lead directly to a tremendous increase in our safety and security, both public and private.

In exactly the same way that every person's carelessly discarded gum wrappers and other "trivial" litter will add up over time and create a trash pile that can't be ignored or tolerated, every person's "trivial" contribution of hostile language adds to the total for society. Every individual decision *not* to add to the linguistic toxic waste dump matters.

SECOND BENEFIT: BETTER HEALTH, AT LESS COST

I wouldn't want you to think that the cost of physical violence is the entire cost of hostile language, however. What you pay for the consequences of physical abuse is only the top of the garbage pile, the dirtiest and therefore most obvious part. Here's another set of facts for your examination.

19

- "Angry, cynical people are five times as likely to die under 50 as people who are calm and trusting . . ." (Redford B. Williams, quoted in Blakeslee, 1989).

- "The data have been there for years: People with close, stable, supportive relationships live longer and suffer less illness than loners" (Yankelovich & Gurin, 1989).

- "Scientists have long noted an association between social relationships and health. More socially isolated or less socially integrated individuals are less healthy, psychologically and physically, and more likely to die" (House et al., 1988).

- "Communication is vitally linked to our bodies and is probably the single most important force that influences our health or lack of health. . . . There is no cause of death that does not kill people who are lonely at significantly higher rates than those who had satisfying lives with others" (James Lynch, in Ornstein & Swencious, 1990).

- "People who are cynical or have hostile attitudes or suppressed anger have been found to have more atherosclerosis and blockage of coronary arteries. And they are more likely to experience heart attacks" (Justice, 1987).

The evidence (available to us for the first time because of today's powerful computers) is overwhelming. We know now that the major risk factors for all diseases and disorders are *exposure to chronic hostility, most of which is verbal, and loneliness*. And because there is no surer way to become lonely than to be hostile, the two are closely linked.

Because the risk is *exposure* to chronic hostility, hostile language is just as dangerous to the person attacked as it is to the attacker. All it takes to make you sick is one person whose tongue keeps you in constant turmoil or one person who is constantly under the lash of *your* tongue—a spouse or a parent will do nicely. If you are someone who's not directly involved in the hostile language but is constantly an audience for it—like the children of fighting parents or the colleagues of a verbally victimized employee, neither of whom feel free to leave the scene of the argument—that will also serve. The damage has little to do with the specific words used. Constant sarcasm, constant belittling, constant nagging, are just as dangerous as the constant shouted obscenities that are more common as part of a pattern of *physical* abuse. The majority of physical assaults are still limited to big cities, but hostile language is *everywhere*.

The next time you find yourself involved in an argument, stop and pay close attention to how your body is reacting. That pounding in your chest is your heart, getting you ready to go on to the next step, which it assumes will be "flight or fight." That queasy feeling in your stomach is your digestive system, hunkering down for combat conditions. The twitching muscle in your cheek, the iron band tightening around your head, your tightly clenched fists . . . all of that is your body answering your brain's call to arms.

The human brain can't tell the difference between a "real" perception from the outside world and one that is only vividly imagined (like the ripe lemon you only imagine biting into, that nevertheless makes your cheeks ache). The messages your brain sends to the rest of your body in confrontations—when your boss or spouse starts chewing you out (or vice versa), when a stranger pushes ahead of you in a line and dares you to do something about it, when your kids defy you openly in a restaurant, when an associate decides to have fun by taunting you in public about your weight or your opinions—are the same messages it would send if you were facing a thug with a knife. Some of us get more upset than others do, some of us feel threatened by a wider variety of things than others do, but the basics are universal: Many times a day, our minds put our bodies on red alert—just in case. And every time it happens, there's a price to pay in wear and tear on your body, your mind, and your spirit.

This barrage of physical effects, a sort of chemical draft notice, has its roots in the most ancient parts of your brain and has changed very little over the millennia. That's why the audiences for hostile language are in danger along with the direct participants. There was no way to be sure that the saber-toothed tiger would leap on your prehistoric neighbor who was its most obvious prey; if you were close by, it might decide to jump on you instead, and you had to be ready to kill it or outrun it. Your brain operates on that basis and asks questions later.

If you are someone who goes through every confrontation looking as cool and calm as if you were alone and at your ease, don't let that confuse you. It only means that you're trained to respond to threatened conflict by imposing a control so tight and so fierce that all the normal surface signs of unease, are suppressed. This creates a tremendous stress on you, both physically and mentally. Your blood pressure will be just as high, your heart and stomach just as likely to suffer. It may in fact be worse for you, because the effort of imposing that control puts additional stress on your body and mind.

The health consequences of hostile language (in addition to those from physical violence, already discussed) are heart attack and ulcer, depression and drug dependency, migraine and psoriasis, power tool accidents and alcoholism—every kind of illness and disorder and impairment and trauma—all due to the normal reactions of your body/mind when you perceive yourself to be threatened. Plus the poor work performance, strained marriages, and less-than-adequate parenting that go along with such conditions. We pay for these consequences right out of our own personal pockets and bank accounts.

We also pay for the days of work missed when we're sick or hurt, for our low productivity when we're well enough to go to work but not well enough to function properly, and for the effect it has on our colleagues when they have to put up with our bad moods and jangled nerves. Employers pay the price for all their employees' problems of this kind as well as for their own—and of course they add that expense to the prices charged for their products or services! What goes around comes around, always.

Taking care of our language environment by keeping it wholesome instead of toxic would cut all these costs dramatically—not only the financial costs, but all the others that go with sickness or injury.

THIRD BENEFIT: GREATER SUCCESS, FOR OURSELVES AND OUR CHILDREN

We have established that two immediate personal benefits of getting rid of hostile language would be greater security and better health, for less than what we now pay, which would mean not only a better quality of life but also tremendous financial savings. That's worth having; that's worth making an effort for. But there's more.

In *Time Magazine* (Gibbs, 1995) Daniel Goleman explains that "IQ gets you hired, but EQ gets you promoted"; his book, *Emotional*

Intelligence (1995), presents his evidence and arguments for that claim. Good technical and intellectual skills and good test scores will still get you a job. But *succeeding* in that job, moving ahead in it—even just keeping it—now depend on emotional skills. These skills are your ability to control your feelings, to put off instant pleasure for long-term good, to understand and "read" other people, to make yourself understood and respected . . . your "EQ."

In the days when most jobs were long term and career changes beyond the age of thirty were almost unknown, there was time and leisure for everyone in a workplace to get to know everybody else and learn one another's quirks and foibles. If a man or woman was hard to get along with, there was time to find out why, to learn to get around the problem, even to try to help. That era is over; so far as anyone can tell, it's over for good. Today we live in the world of "downsizing" and "outsourcing." Successful people today have to be able to move from job to job, from career to career, at the drop of a hat, and they have to *fit in immediately* as part of the team wherever they find themselves.

People who can't do this can get hired, but they don't thrive. They get laid off (in today's most popular term, their companies "shed" them, as if they were dead leaves or dandruff) or they get shuffled into dead-end slots where their only choice is to stagnate or quit. Often they are the flashy ones at first, the people that employers hire with the highest of hopes because they seem to have so much energy, so much fire, such high potential—but they don't last.

This matters for you personally because it can determine your earnings and your status for your entire working life. Furthermore, even if you've gone so far in your field that your own progress at work is no longer a concern for you, you'll still pay. Because your teenage and adult children are just starting out in the world, they don't have your track record, and the EQ-filter applies to *them* in a way it may never apply to you.

What this means for all of us is very simple: If the kids we care about don't have the necessary social and emotional skills to make it in today's workplaces, we can forget about a comfortable retirement. We will either pay what it costs to subsidize them as long as we live, or we will pay what it costs us emotionally to stand by and let people we love do without the things they genuinely need. (In the latter

23

case, we will also dramatically increase the chances that when we are old and need them around, they won't be there.) The "boomerang" kids of today are accurately named. They leave home the same way we did, but they go out into a radically different world, discover that they can't make it out there, and come right back. We can of course throw them out again and tell them to sink or swim, but it won't be free; we're just postponing the bill.

Financial security today depends on the ability to interact well with other people. Those whose standard mode for dealing with others is hostile language, or who don't know how to deal with the hostile language of others effectively, are severely handicapped—and that has a high cost. You can avoid it by getting rid of hostile language.

FOURTH BENEFIT: A LEGACY FOR THE FUTURE

I've left this for last because—unlike greater security, better health, and increased success—it is not direct and obvious and immediate. It probably wouldn't be enough, by itself, to convince people to take better care of the language environment. However, when it's added to the other three, I believe we can accurately say "Case closed!" The fourth benefit comes from the fact that your language behavior is the *model* for the young people who are watching you and listening to you.

You can't just say, "I grew up when it was okay to use language like land mines and it's too late for me to change, but my kids will do better." That's very unlikely. Children are often strongly opposed to talking like their parents, and they may bend over backwards not to use their parents' vocabularies or repeat their parents' jokes and stories, but they learn their language *strategies* by observing the adults they grow up with. If hostile language is your standard method for handling conflict, for getting others to do what you want or need, for persuading others to agree with you, for presenting your plans and ideas, your children will inherit that from you. And it will do them enormous harm—indeed there is strong evidence that verbal abuse is in fact *more* harmful to kids than all but the most grotesque physical abuse. And then, with very few exceptions, they will grow up and install the same communication system in their own homes, where they will hand it on down to *their* children, and so on ad infinitum.

That's not good. If one family maintains a toxic language environment, and its three children grow up believing that that's appropriate, there will probably be three more such families in the next generation. This sets up a cycle of ever-increasing linguistic pollution. At some point we have to stop, or the cycle will destroy us all; we're just now beginning to see its effects. The old joke, "Oh, no! I'm turning into my father (or mother)!" is as accurate as it is clichéd. We've all had the experience of getting into a verbal struggle and suddenly realizing that what was coming from our mouth was our *parent's* voice and words. When we're children and our parents say hostile things to us or to one another, we think "When I grow up, I will *never* say that!" And then the day comes when we are deeply angry with our spouse or child and we suddenly hear ourselves saying exactly those things we were so sure we would never say.

The process of breaking this cycle has to begin somewhere. If you decide that it will start with you, you not only make things better for future generations, you also get those other three payoffs discussed earlier in the chapter. That's not bad; not bad at all.

HE SAYS/SHE SAYS

The media have been flooded in recent years with claims that men and women "speak different languages" and "grow up in different worlds"; John Gray's best-selling *Men Are From Mars, Women Are From Venus* took that idea to its extreme limits. In my opinion, these claims can't be supported, but many people disagree with me. It's important, therefore, to talk briefly about whether the matters taken up in this and other chapters must be custom-tailored for the two genders. Let's take a look at the benefits discussed above to see how they apply to men and to women, and to set out any differences and similarities as clearly as possible.

GENDER AND SAFETY

Women are traditionally perceived as more vulnerable to violence than men. Where nonfatal physical injuries are concerned, the statistics bear that out, but when you go beyond nonfatal injuries to injuries that kill, the rates are far higher for men. Verbal violence, because it doesn't depend on muscles and brawn, is a hostility resource equally available to both sexes. If men have a slight advantage in physical strength (less impressive now that many women are armed), women have a slight advantage in verbal virtuosity. And both genders have to bear the financial costs of functioning in our violent society, paying the bills for insurance and law enforcement and all the rest. Violence is an equal opportunity burden.

However, the potential for turning this around is also gender-neutral. The negatives just described apply only to a context in which most people, whatever their gender, have had little or no training in methods for defusing hostilities while they're still verbal. There is no evidence at all to indicate that either gender is better able to use language to resolve conflicts safely. As a teacher of verbal self-defense for more than two decades, I have never had to modify the training to fit either gender, nor have I ever found a verbal self-defense technique for which I've had to say that one gender was "just naturally better at it" than the other.

GENDER AND HEALTH

The negative health consequences of hostile language apply equally to both genders; the minor differences that do exist cancel one another out and the result is balance. Variations (that is, whether chronic exposure to hostility results in heart disease, cancer, clinical depression, alcoholism, or something else) are clearly individual, not due to gender. Men have more severe physical reactions during intense arguments, which means that a man's very common "I can't TALK about it any longer!" is a plea that should be taken seriously. Women are more likely to brood and torment themselves about arguments that are over, often long after the men involved have completely forgotten the confrontations; for them the analogous plea is, "I can't just FORGET it in ten minutes the way YOU can!" The two sexes are equally vulnerable to all the diseases and disorders that result from toxic language, and equally able to take advantage of the health benefits that result from getting rid of it.

GENDER AND SUCCESS

There are real differences here, but again they balance out. Whatever your gender, the ability to communicate effectively is your most important workplace skill. Because bias against women's speech is still prevalent in our society, and because women's voices are so often perceived as less "adult" than men's voices, women have to work harder to make their language skills pay off. On the other hand, women are somewhat better both at understanding others' body language and at using nonverbal communication themselves, which gives them an advantage.

GENDER AND THE FAMILY FUTURE

No one would claim that the ability to bring up children who are highly skilled at effective communication benefits one gender more than the other. Both mothers and fathers become grandparents, and they are equally anxious to see their offspring down through the generations safe, healthy, happy, and *independently* successful.

It's now clear that there are three significant and *immediate* incentives for good stewardship of the language environment, plus one future benefit thrown in to sweeten the deal. This brings us to our next question: Is hostile language, despite its negative consequences, *necessary*? We all know that getting rid of lightning would spare us a lot of inconvenience, not to mention actual damage to ourselves and to our property. But lightning is a major source of nitrogen for this planet's soil; without lightning strikes to the ground, we would probably starve. Even if we *could* get rid of lightning, we couldn't get along without it. In the next chapter we'll consider whether hostile language is like lightning: dangerous, something we'd like to avoid if we could, but necessary to our lives.

2

IS HOSTILE LANGUAGE
NECESSARY?

Many times throughout history we humans have put projects into place because we could see their immediate benefits, only to find out much later that those benefits were outweighed by negative side effects we hadn't foreseen. Before we consider making the changes in our language behavior that a wholesome language environment would require, we need to decide whether it's possible to offer a rational *defense* of hostile language—something more solid than just "I get a kick out of it!" We need to consider whether hostile language provides us with benefits that are *more* valuable than greater security, better health, and increased success; we need to ask if hostile language, toxic as it is, is so necessary to our lives that we can't afford to get rid of it.

THE ARGUMENTS *FOR* HOSTILE LANGUAGE

When people argue in favor of hostile language or against eliminating it from our lives, or both, their arguments usually are like these four examples:

✦ *We can't transmit negative messages without hostile language.*

People have to be given negative messages—"You didn't pass," "Your experiment was flawed," "You aren't getting your research grant," "Your tumor is malignant," "Your child is using drugs." For such messages, hostile language is often the best (or the only) communication resource.

✦ *We can't motivate people and keep them on track without hostile language.*

Human beings are basically self-indulgent and weak, and they urgently need discipline if they are to accomplish anything in their lives. Without hostile language it's impossible to motivate them and keep them motivated.

✦ *Because human beings are born hostile, trying to get rid of hostile language is ridiculous; it can't be done.*

Attempts to eliminate hostile language are foolish and doomed in advance to failure, because human beings are innately hostile; they can no more give up hostility than they could give up eating.

✦ *We can't give up hostile language because it keeps us from going on to hostile actions.*

Hostile language is necessary because it lets us get rid of our innate hostility without doing serious damage to one another—it serves as an escape valve.

Are any or all of these ideas—which lead almost inescapably to the conclusion that hostile language is as wholesome and natural as breathing—accurate? Many people believe that the answer is yes, and they don't hesitate to say so or to demonstrate their agreement by their behavior.

THOSE WHO SAY YES

Scholar Jonathan Rauch (author of *Kindly Inquisitors: The New Attack on Free Thought*) strongly supports the claim that we have to have hostile language to carry negative messages, and he goes farther than most in openly stating his position. In his article titled "The Humanitarian Threat to Free Inquiry" (*Reason*, April 1993), he writes:

> A very dangerous principle is now being established as a social right: Thou shalt not hurt others with words. This principle is a menace—and not just to civil liberties. At bottom it threatens liberal inquiry—that is, science itself.

Rauch has no sympathy for people who perceive themselves as having been harmed by others' words, and he tells the rest of us how to set such people straight:

> The standard answer to people who say they are offended should be: "Is there any casualty other than your feelings? Are you or others being threatened with violence or vandalism? No? Then it's a shame your feelings are hurt, but that's too bad. You'll live."

You want benefits? Well, he says, what you get from using hostile language and letting others use it without protest is Western science and technology. If it weren't for hostile language we'd still be living in caves, eating our bugs and lizards raw.

Rauch may stand alone in offering an open argument for hostile language based on the claim that Western civilization would be doomed without it. But the four basic positions listed above have plenty of support elsewhere.

Hostile Language and the Law

Our legal system supports hostile speech in many ways, and not just in the sense that we have a constitutional right to free speech. We have no *law* against verbal abuse. There are special linguistic crimes like libel and slander and perjury, intended to prevent *false* language, but no law prohibits hurtful language.

If you are slender and I write an article or give a speech claiming that you're enormously fat, you can sue me for that because it's false. But if you *are* enormously fat, I can say so in public and to your face, as often as I like, no matter how much pain you say it causes you.

If I hit you with a brick and at the same time call you a "stupid redneck," I can be arrested and tried for the physical assault, and the "stupid redneck" epithet can be brought in as evidence of my intention to do you harm. If I tell you that the way you look in your tight sweater drives me crazy and I intend to get you into bed whether you want to be there or not, you can use those words as evidence in a sexual harassment lawsuit against me. But in every case, *the hostile language has to be part of some other legally recognized crime.* The only chargeable offense that comes even remotely close to verbal abuse is "the intentional infliction of emotional distress," an example of which would be a criminal killing someone you love while you are forced to watch.

Hostile Language and Medicine

Verbally abusive doctors, seemingly oblivious to the massive evidence of the power that language has to heal or harm, are so common that people at parties gather in groups to trade their Malpractice Of The Mouth horror stories. ("You think that's bad? Hah! Let me tell you what my doctor said to me!") And we know how doctors develop this habit of ugly talk: More than 80 percent of medical students report that they are subject to frequent verbal abuse all through medical school. The model that much of medical education provides for doctors-in-training is one of unrelenting sarcasm, brow-beating, and vicious criticism. How else, I've been asked by many doctors (and medical professors) over the years, could they get patients and staff to do as they're told?

There are whole systems of therapy based on the premise that people who are hurt by others' words are at best emotionally not up to standard and should seek treatment for their deficiency. Often the judgment is that such people are "neurotic" or worse. The message is the ancient "Sticks and stones will break your bones, but words will never hurt you"—and if you think they <u>will</u>, you need expert help.

Hostile Language, Discipline, and Motivation

Parents assure me that there's no way they can get through to their kids without using hostile language; teachers tell me that control of the classroom absolutely requires it. Employers and supervisors, despite massive evidence that punishment is the poorest of motivational tools, insist that without hostile language in the workplace nothing would ever get done properly. Law enforcement officers inform me that hostile language is one of the most essential tools of their profession.

Much of our military training, especially in the military academies, views hostile language not only as acceptable but as the cornerstone of the training process. "An Officer, Not a Gentleman" (Smolowe, 1993) quotes military sociologist Charles Moskoe talking about men in the military and warning that "you can't oversocialize them because that might even drive out the best pilots."

I once came upon a little boy who was torturing a cat, with tears running down his face. I took the cat away and asked him why he was hurting it, when it so obviously distressed him to do so. He said, "I HAVE to! I'm supPOSED to be able to DO this!" Many people are like that child: They are convinced that they are "supposed to be able" to inflict pain and won't be accepted by their superiors or their peers if they can't.

Stephen King, unchallenged expert at creating fictional portrayals of violence in both word and deed, claims that it's a public service, because as long as we get plenty of that stuff in our entertainment diet we are much less likely to go hunting for it in the real world. In *Danse Macabre* King writes that he sees the most violent examples of the horror genre as "lifting a trapdoor in the civilized forebrain and throwing a basket of raw meat to the hungry alligators swimming around in the subterranean river beneath. Why? Because it keeps them from getting out, man" (King, 1981).

Hostile Language and Human Nature

So—many powerful individuals and groups are either strongly in favor of hostile language, or value it enough to be willing to tolerate its consequences in order to preserve it. Is that because getting rid of it is impossible? Can the case be made that hostile language is a distinguishing mark of our humanity? Are we unable to help ourselves because we are genetically predisposed to be violent? Gerry Spence, in *How to Argue and Win Every Time*, writes that we are "a severely retarded species. In essence we remain the brute, for when confronted the brute attacks, and when faced with need or desire it takes by force from the weaker members of the hierarchy." Is he right?

The problem with this idea is the massive evidence against it. Studies of children as young as six months of age have proved that we are not born hostile at all. When a child barely able to crawl hears another child crying in distress, the first child's reaction is to offer comfort; if that fails, to get a grownup or older child to help; and if *that* fails, to begin crying along with the other child. The only exception to this pattern is in little ones from abusive homes, whose reaction is to *scream at or hit* the child who's crying. This is unquestionably learned behavior. And so is killing on the battlefield.

In his book on that subject (*On Killing: The Psychological Cost of Learning to Kill in War and Society*), Lt. Col. Dave Grossman explains that the innate resistance human beings have to killing other human beings was a serious problem in past wars, where up to 85 percent of our soldiers fired their guns into the air, didn't fire them at all, or found some other way to avoid killing. We have found ways, in more recent wars, to get around some of this resistance, but it isn't easy; it takes intensive effort and considerable time. And we have still found no way to cope with the pain our veterans suffer after the war is over and they have to live with their memories.

Clearly much of our society is convinced that whatever the costs of violence, we cannot do without it. Never mind that I have the Catholic Bishops on my side; they and I appear to be in the minority. And never mind the scholars and experts; we don't have to rely on them for evidence of our attitudes. In almost any home where there are children, dialogues like these have taken place or will take place:

34

***

CHILD: "Hey, Tommy won't <u>play</u> with me any more!"

PARENT: "Did you hit him? Did you take a toy away from him?"

CHILD: "No! We were just <u>talk</u>ing! And I called him a baby and now he won't <u>play</u> with me!"

PARENT: "Is that all? Oh, well . . . don't worry about it. He'll get over it."

***

CHILD: "How come Aunt Jennifer isn't eating with us? Is she sick?"

PARENT: "Naah. You know how your aunt is . . . she's always getting her feelings hurt. She'll get over it."

That's a clear message to the children: When people are hurt by your words, kids, that's *their* problem. Perhaps that's how the executives among my clients came to the same conclusion.

WHY THOSE WHO SAY YES ARE MISTAKEN

In the face of all this, you may be wondering: How can I go on arguing that we must eliminate hostile language from our lives? Let me say first of all that I agree with the bishops that hostile language is sinful, but I'm thinking of a different sin. They were concerned with hostile language as evidence of cruelty, of sadism, of a desire to wound and damage others. I will come back to that issue when we take up hostile language in the home, and show you that in adults such language is almost never due to a desire to cause pain. That common misconception is responsible for much unnecessary suffering. But there certainly is a sin involved, and it's one of the Big Seven "deadly" ones: the sin of *sloth*.

Rauch and all the others might be right if hostile language were the only language I could use to tell you that you had failed your exams or that your evidence in your scientific experiment was flawed or that you were going to be fired—any of the infinite variety of negative messages that life requires us to deliver. They might be right if no other effective way existed for convincing adults to show up for work on time, children to do their homework, soldiers and teams to work together toward common objectives. But it's not like that; our resources are not that limited.

Hostile and hurtful language is neither the only way to deliver such messages, nor the most effective or efficient way. It's just the *easy* way. It's the way that comes most quickly to mind and requires the least thought and effort, just as opening your back door and flinging your trash out into the yard is. It is, in short, the *lazy*—slothful—way. There are other ways, if you are willing to use them. For a quarter of a century I have been teaching people how to deliver negative messages in a positive manner, and I assure you that the only barrier to doing so is laziness.

The idea that we must have hostile language to preserve our liberties, motivate our workers, and so on, can be defended if and only if there is no adequate alternative. I'm going to demonstrate to you that we have alternatives that are not only adequate but superior, that we're all able to take advantage of them, and that far from being "the brute," we are fully capable of learning to set brutality aside and carry on our lives successfully without it.

As emergency physician Ellen Taliaferro (Liles, 1994) points out: Even if it could be proved that some of us are born violent, "we're also born incontinent, and we're expected to get over that by the time we reach school age."

We have been sold a sleazy bill of goods proposing that gentle language is only for wimps, that getting ahead in this world depends on using your tongue like a bullwhip, and that—just in case we aren't convinced by either of those arguments—there's no point in trying to behave differently anyway, because human beings are *born* violent and we can't help ourselves.

In the chapters ahead I will show you that that's all wrong. I'll show you an assortment of typical incidents from our daily lives in which we would tend either to use hostile language or to choke it back and feel ashamed because we perceive that as cowardice. I will demonstrate to you that far better and more honorable ways to handle such situations exist, and that there is nothing hostile language can achieve that cannot be achieved in other, more wholesome, ways.

SHE SAYS/HE SAYS

Are there real gender differences with regard to the issues discussed in this chapter? As is true for every aspect of male/female communication, this is a matter of dispute even among the experts. I will give you my opinion, based on my research, my quarter century of experience in the field, and my own life. To discuss it sensibly, however, we have to discuss it in the context of physical violence. Because verbal violence is where physical violence starts; the two cannot be separated.

Many sources state that most physical violence is done by males while most verbal violence is done by females. Our socialization process, in which little girls are trained to be "nice" and constantly told that nice little girls don't hit, makes that plausible. But that claim, whether true or not in the statistical sense, misses the point—because the difference is due not to gender but to power. In most disagreements that become violent, the man is physically stronger than the woman and is therefore freer to do physical harm without fear of being paid back in kind. But he would feel the same freedom in an argument with a physically weaker man; and when the woman is the stronger of the two, the man is as unlikely to hit as a woman would be.

There *is* a gender difference in the verbal messages delivered when hostile language escalates to physical abuse, and when those who hit are asked, afterward, to explain why. This difference directly reflects a set of beliefs about male/female relationships.

Abused women consistently report being hit by male partners who then say, "LOOK what you made me DO!" or "WHY did you make me DO that?" People who work with male batterers consistently report being told "I only did what I <u>had</u> to do" and "Men are <u>supposed</u> to be in charge of the family" and "If she'd do what she's <u>supposed</u> to do, I wouldn't <u>have</u> to hit her!" In *Pragmatics of Com-*

37

munication, Paul Watzlawick (1967) describes a man among his patients who sums it all up superbly well: When his wife was able to convince him that he was factually wrong during an argument, he said, "Well, you may be right, but you're still <u>wrong</u>, because you're arguing with <u>me</u>!" That is, she may be *factually* right, but he considers her *morally* wrong.

Men are still learning, as children, that it's their duty and responsibility to be in charge. Add that to the belief that violence is acceptable when it can't be avoided, mix in the mistaken idea that no other alternatives for managing conflict are available, and you have a reliable recipe for violence. The only question is whether the violence will be confined to language or will escalate to physical abuse; in either case, harm will be done.

This particular gender difference in the use of hostile language simply reflects the fact that men are the ones identified as the dominant gender in this power ethic. It's not that only men *believe* it, although men may be more consciously aware that they do. I have heard many women say of verbally abusive male partners, "Well, at least he never <u>hits</u> me!" I have heard women as well as men say that a particular case of physical violence was understandable because the woman hit "was asking for it"; they say, "What did she <u>expect</u>?" Little girls too young to worry about being politically correct, asked whether it's okay for a boy to hit a girl, will say, "It depends—what did she <u>do</u>?" It goes all the way back to Becky Thatcher being told that when Tom Sawyer dunks her braids in the inkwell it proves his affection for her, and beyond. And women who adamantly insist that they reject the whole thing can often be observed applying it in their behavior toward their children, who are of course weaker than they are.

No purpose is served by trying to sweep this under the rug and pretend that only men believe it. As long as this set of beliefs is shared at some level by many individuals of both genders, it will continue to thrive in our society. It has to be brought out into the light and dealt with.

PART TWO

LAYING THE FOUNDATION

3

DETACHMENT

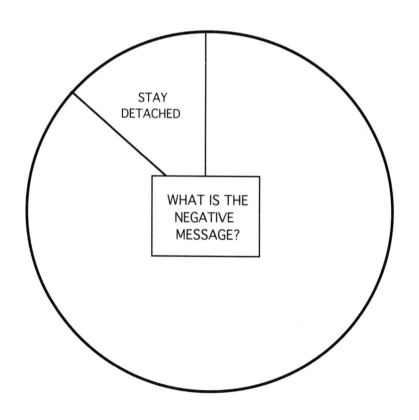

STAY
DETACHED

WHAT IS THE
NEGATIVE
MESSAGE?

Scenario A

Ellen walked through the front door ten minutes after Jack did. He wasted no time before letting her know how he felt about that.

"Where have you been?" he demanded, both hands on his hips and his face set in a fierce scowl. "You were supposed to be home half an hour ago, for crying out loud!"

Ellen stared at him. "What do you mean, where have I been? I've been at work!"

"Oh, don't give me that!," he snapped. "You get off at five, Ellen, and it's nearly six-thirty! You've been in some store, haven't you?"

"I had to stop for milk, Jack! I can't go out in the backyard and pick it, you know, I have to get it at the store!"

"If you'd sit down and make a grocery list at the beginning of the week like I keep telling you to, you wouldn't run out of something every single day! If I ran my business the way you run this house—"

"If you did your share of running this house, Jack, I might listen to that! But you don't! I hold down a full-time job just like you do, and then I come home and have all the housework to do on top of it, while you stand around and complain!"

"Oh, come on, Ellen," Jack said, sarcasm dripping from every word, "there's no comparison between my job and yours, and you know it! You sit around at that office all day reading magazines and filing your nails—I really work! And when I get home, I expect a little hard-earned peace and relaxation! But YOU can't even get home in time to cook DINner!"

Ellen was still standing in the door, still wearing her coat; she was as white as a sheet.

"Well?," he demanded. "What do you have to say for yourself?"

"Just . . . one . . . thing!," she spat at him. "Thank heaven we don't have a child! At least I'm the only one around here that has to put up with your vicious mouth!"

Jack caught his breath; now he was as white as she was. "Oh, man," he said softly. "You really know how to <u>hurt</u> a guy, <u>don't</u> you, Ellen?"

WHAT'S GOING ON HERE?

This is combat, plain and simple. Jack and Ellen are an ordinary couple with ordinary problems, but a lot of what passes for communication at their house is the linguistic equivalent of machine gun fire and hand grenades. And it just keeps getting worse.

POINTS OF VIEW

The way Ellen sees it, Jack takes pleasure in causing her pain. Nothing she does is ever good enough to deserve his praise; no mistake is ever minor enough for him to let it pass. She is convinced that he gets up in the morning and plans his day around his chances to chew her out and make her miserable. It baffles her. He claims that he loves her and she has plenty of reasons to believe that he's telling the truth; in other ways, he's a good and obviously caring husband. *Why*, then, does he get so much joy out of attacking her? It hurts her so much when he starts his verbal abuse that she can't even *think* straight!

*****

The way Jack sees it, Ellen is just like the people he works with. Like them, she gives him no respect, and when he tries to help, she acts as if he were stupid. What he really wants is a loving and peaceful home where he and Ellen can find companionship and have a good life together. But she won't help, and she acts as if he has no right even to make suggestions—she gets her feelings hurt over every little thing he says, and when she gets mad she goes out of her way to attack him where she knows he is most vulnerable. It baffles him; *why* can't she cooperate once in a while? Why can't they sit down together and discuss their problems—for example, how to divide up the housework—like two rational adults? It's bad enough always being low man in the pecking order at work, without coming home and getting the cold shoulder there too! Ellen claims to love him, and in lots of ways she's a wonderful wife, but that only makes it harder to understand. It's like getting cut with a knife, listening to the things she says and seeing the way she looks at him—it hurts him so much that he can't even *think* straight!

This is communication breakdown; it's far too typical, and far too frequent. Both Ellen and Jack, once an argument begins, are in so much pain from what they perceive as the other's determination to *hurt* them that they say (or yell) anything that comes into their heads, and never mind the consequences. In a language environment like this one, the hurts pile up and fester, and matters quickly go from bad to worse to unbearable. When Jack and Ellen have had time to think, they're sorry for the things they said and wonder how they could have said them, but it's too late. Whether this kind of fighting is between husband and wife, boss and employee, parent and child, or any other two people, when the verbal combat is like Ellen and Jack's—a blind and frantic flailing away to see who can do the most damage fastest—communication simply stops. How can this happen between well-intentioned people who are genuinely fond of each other?

It happens because neither person involved has the detachment that has to be there if they are to react rationally instead of emotionally.

Detachment is almost impossible to fake; it has to be real. When people undergo what Daniel Goleman calls "an emotional hijacking"—when a sequence of language sets off an alarm in the amygdala (the area of the brain that's always on guard for that purpose) before it can get to the thinking part—they don't have enough control even to try to pretend. Detachment can only be present when there is no highly emotional response to provoke the hijacking.

It may seem to you that a neutral reaction to hostile language is impossible. Understanding *why* people turn to hostile speech is the key; for the most part, this is something that people *mis*understand. Let's take a careful look at the phenomenon.

WHY PEOPLE BECOME CHRONIC
USERS OF HOSTILE LANGUAGE

Everybody uses hostile language once in a while. You've had a terrible day, you're worn out, you've put up with one ridiculous situation after another all day long, you've already got a headache, and suddenly you simply "*lose* it." Your spouse or a friend or one of your kids asks you an innocuous question and instead of answering it you find yourself ranting and raving and yelling and carrying on. That happens to everybody now and then, the way tripping over something happens to everybody. It requires no explanation; it's part of being human.

Unfortunately, however, for an ever-growing part of our population hostile language isn't just a rare loss of control, quickly regretted and easily understood. Instead, it's frequent and routine and chronic; often it forms a substantial part of the individual's language activity every single day. This is dangerous for the hostile speaker and for everyone he or she interacts with, and it *does* require explanation. We can't deal with it effectively if we don't understand what's going on, because effective communication in such circumstances requires us to keep our heads and maintain enough detachment to stay aware of what we're saying and why we're saying it. We can do it only if we know why this kind of no-holds-barred verbal combat happens, and why it seems to be getting worse all the time.

The conventional wisdom about adult hostile language—people use it to hurt other people—is short, to the point, and almost always *wrong*. Sure, a sadist will use language as one of an array of methods for causing pain, but sadists are very rare and very sick. You're not likely to run into more than one in an entire lifetime, and understanding sadism is a task best left to highly trained experts in mental illness. Instead, the question we should concern ourselves with is: Why do many *normal* people, mentally stable ordinary people like ourselves, routinely use hostile language?

Chronic users of hostile language fall into three general categories:

Type 1   Those who are unaware that any other method for handling disagreement exists.

45

Type 2   Those for whom verbal hostility fills a strong personal need for excitement that they don't know how to fill adequately in other ways.

Type 3   Those for whom verbal hostility fills a strong personal need for human attention that they don't know how to fill adequately in other ways.

(There are of course also people who are a combination of these three basic types.)

In all these cases, the basic problem isn't wickedness; the most negative term we can reasonably use is *ignorance*. Almost always, the problem is a lack of awareness of the communication resources that are available—a lack of essential information.

TYPE 1: THOSE WHO ARE UNAWARE OF ALTERNATIVES FOR HANDLING DISAGREEMENT

Most people would prefer to get through life without having to fight every single step of the way; they feel a need for at least a moderate amount of peace in their lives. To achieve this goal, they want ways to deal with the inevitable disagreements that they face as human beings. If they are unaware of other methods for handling disagreement, hostile language becomes their conflict resolution mechanism. It doesn't work very well, of course, but if they know of no alternative they will continue to use it. It has nothing at *all* to do with being cruel or enjoying others' pain. People in this group are usually very glad to change their language behavior—and very quick to do so—once they've been made aware of the linguistic resources available to them.

When people reach adulthood without ever having learned any *positive* ways to resolve conflict, they are likely to tackle it with hostile language in spite of its negative consequences. Especially if, as is typical for youngsters growing up in recent years, they've had no contact with a model of wholesome communication that would give them reason to believe other choices exist.

When I was a small child, I had many opportunities to observe people in language interactions of all kinds. My family sat down every night to a shared meal and shared conversation. People sat out on their porches in the evening and on weekends during much of the year and talked; neighbors came over and joined in. There were big family dinners on holidays; there were family picnics on Memorial Day and the 4th of July and Labor Day. Television didn't yet exist, and people didn't sit and eat their meals in front of the radio. I had conversations to observe and learn from every single day and evening, and in the natural way of things I saw a wide variety of *disagreements* happen. I saw adults handle conflict with hostile language, certainly, but I saw other adults handle it in more positive ways, giving me a chance to compare and choose among strategies.

Life in this country has changed drastically since those days. I have no desire to go back to a time before television and air conditioning and polio vaccine, but I would gladly reinstate the language environment of my childhood if I could. For a huge percentage of young people since the 1960s, exposure to real and satisfactory human communication, let alone conversation and discussion, has grown increasingly rare. With so many single-parent families, and so many families where both parents work full time outside the home, regular gatherings for family meals have almost disappeared. In families where everyone *is* home to eat meals together, a common practice is to watch the tv set while eating; this efficiently cuts off communication. No one can expect children to learn conversational skills in our troubled schools, or from the company of their equally inexperienced peers. All too often the only communication model available on a regular basis is the television set—where talk shows demonstrate vicious communication, soap operas demonstrate fantasy communication, and situation comedies hammer down the message that the person with the meanest mouth gets all the laughs and all the goodies.

My first step when I begin work with a private client is to ask for a cassette tape, about half an hour long, that will let me observe that client in conversation. At least a fourth of my clients call me in a few days and tell me they can't provide that tape. They say, "I never realized it before, but I don't <u>have</u> conversations. I have interviews, like at work or at the doctor's office, and I go to meetings, and I do sales pitches, and I have fights—but I don't have conversations. I'm not even sure I know <u>how</u> to have a conversation!"

This is a genuinely sad condition for an adult to be in. What I "prescribe" as a first tentative step out of it is a regular television diet of *Washington Week in Review*, the closest thing to real human conversation that television offers in many parts of the country. And I tell the client, "Do not, under any circumstances, watch *Crossfire* or *The McLaughlin Group*!"

If you are someone who relies on hostile language only because you're unfamiliar with the alternatives, reading this book will go a long way toward solving your problem, because it will provide you with the basic information you need.

TYPE 2: THOSE WHO ARE SEEKING EXCITEMENT

For some people, confronting others with hostile language satisfies a personal need for *excitement*. They enjoy verbal fights as a source of a "rush" or "high," saying things like, "Hey, I really get a <u>kick</u> out of getting other people <u>going</u>!" They're quite frank about this, and very stubborn. They're not willing to give up hostile language, because they view it as a positive part of their lives. Causing pain is not *their* goal, either. They're like people who love to bowl or swim or play tennis; they assume that all rational human beings share their passion for verbal fights (or *would* share it once they saw how much fun it is). They take it for granted that all normal human beings enjoy arguing as much as they do. And when they hear another person object to an argument and complain that it's painful, they immediately decide that the complaint is just a ruse the other person is using as a strategy for winning the argument.

All of this would be fine if they used hostile language only with other consenting adults—people who, like them, really do perceive arguing as a sport. They don't. They seem genuinely unaware that not everyone perceives disagreement as they do, and because in their eagerness to get the match underway they don't stop and listen, they don't learn that they're misinformed.

When these people are asked to pay close attention to what's going on in their bodies at the end of hostile language episodes, they report pounding hearts, racing pulses, sweaty palms, rapid shallow breathing, and a general "shakiness." They experience the physical phenomena that most people experience on airplanes during severe turbulence. But they interpret that state as pleasure and actively seek it out, in the same way that others may seek out physical danger (bungee-jumping, for example) and enjoy *its* physical effects.

This pattern is relatively rare in adults; not as rare as sadistic behavior, but still uncommon. (I have seen it most often in two quite different populations—very young men and elderly women.) These speakers seem to have no experience of the pleasure that comes from being someone that everybody is eager to spend time with. And they are unfamiliar with the satisfaction that goes with being able to perceive and handle verbal conflict in the same way that martial arts experts perceive and handle *physical* conflict.

TYPE 3: THOSE WHO ARE SEEKING HUMAN ATTENTION

Far more common are people who use hostile language as a way of proving to themselves (and sometimes to others) that they have the power to get and hold another person's attention. For them, their target's emotional reaction is evidence of that power, nothing more. These people make up the majority of chronic verbal abusers in every walk of life, and it's a mistake to assume that they use hostile language to cause pain. They've learned that hostile language *does* reliably cause other people to pay attention to them, in the same way that fishermen learn that fish pay more attention to certain kinds of bait than to others. The pain their language causes is, for them, an irrelevant side effect, and one they're willing to tolerate if they must.

The need for attention, the need to feel that other people are not *indifferent* to you, is one of the strongest human needs—so strong that the basic principle verbal abusers follow is "I'd rather be disliked—or worse—than be ignored." We see it in children who, although normally well behaved, will do outrageous things when your preoccupation with guests makes them feel invisible and neglected. We see it in teenagers who know they're unpopular with their peers and who use verbal abuse to make sure that at least those peers can't ignore their existence. This is yet another information gap: These people need to know that there are other and more positive ways to get and hold people's attention.

Most people who are frequent or chronic users of hostile language have no interest in causing pain; it's not their goal. They fit one of the profiles above, or some combination of them. However, their behavior inevitably results in . . .

HOSTILITY LOOPS

All language interactions are *feedback loops*; I base what I say to you on what I understood you to say to me, and vice versa. Arguments like the one in Scenario A are *hostility* loops. The people involved are trapped in the loop, going helplessly around and around, feeding more ammunition and more pain into the loop from both directions with every utterance. Both are convinced that the altercation must end with a winner and a loser, and both feel obligated to win.

However, only a small part of what happens in the loop is due to either person's reaction to the *surface* message that the words would carry if a robot spoke them. Far more of the reaction, often most of it, is to the *emotional* messages: the metamessages about *why* each person is saying what he or she is saying. And if I as listener believe your metamessage is that you want to hurt me—or deceive me or frighten me or control me or make me feel stupid—I'm likely to use hostile language when I respond to you. This is why it's so critically important to understand what ordinarily lies behind hostile language in our society, so that we can avoid leaping to incorrect conclusions about other people's motives and intentions toward us.

Most of the disagreements and conflicts we run into don't happen because we have to face down half a dozen menacing thugs on a mean street. Examples like these are much more likely:

* You're at a party, standing with a small group of people, talking, when one of your friends starts making derogatory statements about Catholics. You feel hypocritical just listening as if you approve of what your friend is saying; you can't just walk away without looking and feeling like a coward. You feel obliged to take a stand and make it clear that you don't endorse your friend's position.

50

- You want to go to Colorado for the family vacation; your spouse wants to go to San Francisco. Your spouse says that only "jocks like you," with no brain and no taste and no education, are interested in Colorado vacations. You don't want to have a fight; you think your spouse has a perfect right to disagree about this matter. But you do want to go to Colorado, not San Francisco. Furthermore, you think the nasty cracks about people like yourself who enjoy sports are elitist and way out of line. You feel that you can't just let them go by; you have to stand up for yourself.

- You're eating dinner at your in-laws' house. Your sister-in-law begins talking about how "everybody knows" that putting kids in daycare ruins their lives, guarantees that they'll be dropouts and criminals, and is evidence of rotten parents who don't take their role seriously. You fully intend to put *your* kids in daycare, you're reasonably certain that she *knows* that, and you feel that she's both mistaken and rude. You hate the idea of spoiling the dinner for your mother- and father-in-law and the other guests. On the other hand, how can you let her get away with something like this? You feel obligated to disagree.

In such situations, the first choice is whether to speak up or keep silent. Most of us, in contexts like these, would like to have a satisfactory way to express our feelings honestly. Unfortunately, people usually do one of two things when they face this choice:

1. They state their case, but they do it using hostile language, which feeds the hostility loop and makes the conflict worse.

2. They keep silent to preserve the peace. But afterward, they despise the other person for putting them in such an awkward position in the first place, and they despise themselves for being such wimps.

Neither choice is a good one, obviously. Nor is it a good choice when a disagreement goes on at great length until someone really *is* whipped by the other person and appears to be the "loser." Or when neither person will give up and accept "defeat" and the argument is carried into the next day (and week, and month) and continued at every possible opportunity, like a blood feud. We need better choices, alternative choices that offer some hope of a *positive* outcome.

STAYING DETACHED

In describing the purposes of hostile language I have concentrated so far on only one side of the interaction. But in each case I've pointed out what it is that the speaker using the hostile language would need to know in order to change his or her ways—as if I thought that I could rely on you, in an interaction with that person, to be interested in filling the information gap, if only as a way to improve your own language environment. That's deliberate; I do think I can rely on you. But only if you understand that the abuser's motivation is *not* to cause you harm.

When someone abuses you with language and you take it for granted that their motive is to hurt you, it's natural for you to react with anger and pain and perhaps fear. Trying to *smother* your anger and pretend a calm you don't feel only turns the negative emotion inward and makes it fester. Pretending won't work; forcing yourself to be courteous through a seething rage won't work. In order to react to such language with the necessary detachment to respond effectively, you have to understand what's really going on:

> *These people aren't out to hurt you. Either they are ignorant of any other method for handling disagreement, or they use hostile language to fill personal needs for excitement and/or human attention and know no other way to satisfy those needs adequately. Even those who consider conversational combat a sport are only looking for a sparring partner; the only way they know to find one is to attack you so that you'll counter-attack and join them in the game.*

Knowing this won't make the language coming at you any less abusive. You won't like it any better than you ever did. However, you won't become hurt or angry, and you'll stay in control of your emotions. It will change your *reaction* to the language, save you from an emotional hijacking, and give you the ability to stop and ask yourself three essential questions and try to answer them:

1. What is the hostile speaker's motivation for talking to me this way?

2. What do I actually disagree with in this case? That is: do I disagree with the speaker's claims, do I think the speaker's facts are wrong, do I object only to the tone the speaker is using, or is it something else?

3. What is the most effective way for me to respond?

When your reaction is immediate outrage and/or pain, you not only won't be able to answer those questions, you won't even remember what the questions *are*.

Achieving this detachment is not as difficult as you might think—you don't have to be "saintly" to do it. As is so often true, the first few times are the hardest, and then it becomes easy. I want to suggest two simple things you can do that often make it easier in the beginning.

Taking Out the Garbage

Step One:

When the hostile episode is over and you have a minute, sit down and write a letter to the other person involved. Write down all the hateful things you would have liked to say at the time, whether you actually did say them or not. You have two goals when you do this. The first is to get all those toxic utterances out of your system so that they don't keep playing over and over in your head like one of those endless-loop music tapes. The second is to externalize the emotion by perceiving it as an external "object"—an object that you're free to do whatever you like with—instead of as something that's inside you and part of you.

Step Two:

Put the letter away in a safe place where no one else will come across it accidentally, and leave it there for at least twenty-four hours.

Step Three:

Take the letter out and read it, reminding yourself that it represents your reaction to someone who is not a sadist or a monster, but merely uninformed and inept. (You may be amazed at how strongly you reacted.)

Step Four:

Destroy the letter, so that no one but you will ever even know that it existed.

This process really does help. It's bad for you to deal with anger by stashing it away inside you and trying to force yourself not to think about it. That's like being told "Don't think about a purple elephant!"; you *will* think about one. Writing it down lets you take out the linguistic garbage so that you can forget about it, without having shoved it under anyone else's nose. Over time your letters will show less evidence of negative emotions and more evidence of detachment; eventually you'll realize that you don't need to write the letters any longer. (And if you are a person who genuinely detests writing, you can substitute a tape recording for the letters and achieve similar results.)

USING THREE-PART SELF-MESSAGES

Effectiveness trainer Thomas Gordon long ago proposed an extremely useful language pattern (based on the traditional "I-message") which he calls a "three-part assertion message." An example of an I-message would be "When you forget to water the tomatoes, I feel angry"; Dr. Gordon added a third part that contains the real-world consequences of such behavior, as in "When you forget to water the tomatoes, I feel angry, because plants die without water." Every part of the message has to be concrete and verifiable in the real world—as in the tomato plant example—and it has to be free of moral judgments.

I know no more effective way to get past the immediate knee-jerk negative reaction that people have to complaints than to use this pattern; it works wonders. In Chapter 9 we'll come back to it and discuss precisely how to use it with other people, which requires you to concern yourself with the verifiability of your message in the external world. But just as you can write a letter and not send it, you can write a three-part message that you have no intention of delivering. In that situation your focus can be on the *internal* world of your own feelings, beliefs, and opinions.

Suppose you go to a party with your spouse, talk to a lot of interesting people, and enjoy yourself tremendously. Suppose that after you get home your spouse turns on you, repeats three or four things you said to others at the party, and shouts, "You said EVERY SINGLE ONE of those things just to make ME feel STUPid!" You're flabbergasted; you had no such motive; you were just enjoying yourself and trying to be good company. After the episode is over, write down a three-part self-message that will clarify your reaction for you and help you find answers to the three questions on page 53. The message is for your eyes only; you write it like this:

Part One:

"When you yelled 'You said EVERY SINGLE ONE of those things just to make ME feel STUPid!' . . ."

What you include in this part of the message should be as exact a quotation of what was said to you as you can make it; don't change it to "When you accused me of X . . ." or do any other revising and interpreting. Just write down the hostile language that you heard.

Part Two:

"I felt . . ."

Fill the blank with your best understanding of exactly what you did feel. "I felt brokenhearted . . ." "I felt furious and betrayed . . ." "I felt as if you'd hit me with your fist . . ." "I felt as if I wanted to hit you with my fist . . ." Again, the message is for you only; never mind how extreme (or how wimpy) it seems to you. Just state your feelings.

Part Three:

    "because I believe that . . ."

Fill the blank with your honest assessment of the reason for your reaction. "Because I believe that what you said was vicious and cruel, and none of it was true." "Because I believe it proves you don't love me." "Because I believe that no decent person would say a thing like that."

As you did with your taking-out-the-garbage letter, put the message away and look at it again the next day to see how you perceive it when you've had a chance to sleep on it. If you then feel that it's all wrong, write a new message and repeat the process. When you're satisfied with your results, throw the message (and any revisions) away. Your goal is to clarify your own reactions, to increase your understanding of what happens when you personally are involved in an episode of hostile language.

It would be absurd to expect people to react with detachment to someone's *physical* violence; even in the rare instances when that would be appropriate, it's something we expect only of saints and therapists. Similarly, if you have firm evidence that someone really *is* a sadist, it's unreasonable to expect you to react to that person's sadistic language with detachment simply because you know sadism is an illness. However, detachment in response to ordinary hostile speech requires neither moral perfection nor medical training. It's easily learned, and it's critically important to cleaning up the language environment.

HE SAYS/SHE SAYS

We give men far more leeway in our culture to act out their feelings of anger than we give women; on the other hand, we give women more freedom to act out feelings of hurt and pain. This means that

56

many men are somewhat more likely to respond to hostile language with an immediate counterattack, while many women are slightly more likely to try to be "nice." But these are only tendencies, and stereotypical tendencies at that; more often than not, they are set aside when disagreements happen in private between intimates.

The only gender difference here that has to be kept in mind is that men, because of the demands our culture lays upon them, often have much more extreme reactions to a loss of face—especially in front of other people—than women do. Men are more likely to go on grimly fighting about something they really don't care about at all, just to avoid the loss of face that they feel would result if they dropped the argument. Anything that will reduce the potential loss of face has a good chance of also reducing the level of hostility. We'll be discussing a number of techniques and strategies for that purpose in this book.

ANOTHER LOOK AT SCENARIO A

Remember Eileen and Jack, in the scenario that opened this chapter? What if one or both of them had been aware of the facts about the purposes for which people use hostile language and had been able to bring detachment to bear? How might the scenario have gone differently? Let's look at some of the possibilities.

The scenario begins when Ellen arrives home ten minutes after her husband and find him waiting to confront her . . .

IF ELLEN STAYS DETACHED

JACK: "<u>Where</u> have <u>you</u> <u>been</u>? You were supposed to be home half an <u>hour</u> ago, for crying out loud!"

ELLEN: "What do you mean, where have I been? I've been at <u>work</u>!"

JACK: "Oh, <u>don't</u> give me that! You get off at <u>five</u>, Ellen, and it's nearly six-thirty! <u>You've</u> been in some <u>store</u>, <u>haven't</u> you?"

ELLEN: "You must have had a horrible day, Jack. Do you want to tell me about it?"

JACK: "It was just the same old thing—just like always. Where've you been?"

ELLEN: "I had to stop for milk. Let me put it away, and then I would be very interested in hearing about today's 'same old thing.' "

JACK: "Naah—I don't want to talk about it" (or, "We can talk about it while we eat").

ELLEN: "That's fine with me. I'll go start dinner, then."

JACK: "Okay. How about if I make the salad?"

If Jack Stays Detached

JACK: "Where've you been, honey? I expected you half an hour ago."

ELLEN: "What do you mean, where have I been? I've been at <u>work</u>!"

JACK: "Ellen, you get off at five and it's nearly six-thirty. I was beginning to wonder."

ELLEN: "I had to stop for milk, Jack! I can't go out in the backyard and <u>pick</u> it, you know. I <u>have</u> to get it at the store!"

JACK: "And the traffic was horrible, and there were fifteen people ahead of you in line at Kroger's, right?"

ELLEN: "Right! And all of them in the <u>express</u> lane, Jack, with a dozen things in their carts! That makes me <u>so</u> <u>mad</u>!"

JACK: "I know what you mean—I always want to make a speech at them."

ELLEN: "I wish you'd been there; I would have cheered you on! But I'm home now—I'll go start dinner."

JACK: "Okay. How about if I make the salad?"

Nothing that happens in either of these revisions requires any deep thinking or subtle planning. In both cases, one person throws out a line or two of hostile language and the other—instead of instantly responding in kind—remains detached and offers a neutral response. Hostility loops have to be fed; they're not self-sustaining. When Jack refuses to provide fuel for the loop, Ellen calms down and drops the hostile language; when it's Ellen who stays neutral, Jack is the one who decides not to go on picking a fight. Nobody loses face in either revision, and nobody's evening is spoiled.

When one partner in the revisions stays detached for a sentence or two, the situation turns around very quickly. It may not always happen that fast outside this book—I'm well aware of that. The more tense and upset the hostile partner is, the longer it may take to lower the emotional intensity. In ordinary circumstances, however, three or four conversational turns should be enough. If it takes longer, that's a clue: It tells you that the circumstances *aren't* ordinary and that some of the techniques coming up in later chapters—in addition to detachment—will be needed.

4

LISTENING

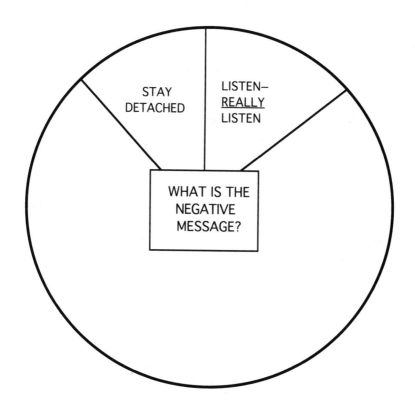

Scenario B

Carl Hayward looked at the meeting agenda, put a checkmark by the item the group had just finished, read the next line, and turned to Martin Blake. "Martin," he said, "it says here that you have an idea for cutting our customer losses in the suburbs. Is that right?"

"Yes, it is," Martin answered. "I know exactly what we ought to do."

"All right," Carl said. "That's something we ought to fix if we can." There was a murmur of agreement from the others around the table; the problem was a long-standing one, and getting worse all the time. "Let's hear what you have in mind."

"It's simple," Martin said, "and it's the obvious right move. All we need is a newsletter for the customers in the suburbs that would fo———"

Carl stared at him, flabbergasted. *Of all the dumb ideas!* "Whoa!," he snapped, cutting Martin off in mid-word; his right hand shot up and out to underline the STOP signal. "Just hold it right there!"

"But, Carl, I haven't even ———"

"Sorry, Martin, it's out of the question! Too expensive — and too much work involved." *I don't know who Blake thought he was going to show off for,* Carl thought, *but he can just do it on his own time.* "Thanks anyway."

"But, Carl, listen, I ———"

"Sorry, Martin," Carl said again, without looking at the other man, his voice cold and distant. "Thanks for your input—it just doesn't happen to be anything we need. Now—let's see what we've got next . . . Oh, yeah! Item 4. According to the figures I saw yesterday, as of April 9th we are beginning to . . ."

WHAT'S GOING ON HERE?

This sort of conflict is all too common today; I see it everywhere. Sometimes it's a simple lack of manners, but often it reflects our obsession with getting everything done *fast*. The problem is that it's the linguistic equivalent of being "penny-wise and pound-foolish"; the minutes we save cost us hours down the road.

POINTS OF VIEW

Martin is angry, and he feels like a fool. He had spent a lot of time getting ready to explain his idea for the newsletter—including the evidence that every dollar spent on it would bring in three dollars in return, and a way to produce it that would take almost no time and almost no in-house writing. He had dug up all the information, he'd run all the figures, and there was no question he wasn't ready to answer. He's confident that he could have made his case if he'd been given half a chance. His perception of the situation is that Carl is a bully who likes to make other people look stupid in public and gets a big kick out of their humiliation.

Martin's mind is made up now. He won't fall for any of Carl's sucker plays ("Would you guys give this some thought and see what you can come up with?") again. From now on, he'll keep his ideas to himself.

*****

Carl is angry, and he's disgusted with Martin. It's true that the suburban customer losses are too high and something needs to be done. But a newsletter? With paper costs sky high and postage going through the roof? Not to mention the problem of who could be spared to *write* it! Carl approves of people who bring up their own ideas. He likes people with initiative, people who are self-starters, and he makes sure his employees know that. But he expects them to propose something solid and logical, something they've put careful thought into, not wild off-the-wall schemes they've just whipped up overnight to show off with.

*****

Carl may be right that the newsletter is a ridiculous idea; on the other hand, it may be the solution he's been searching for for months. He'll never know, because he didn't let Martin talk long enough to get even a minimum amount of information to base a judgment on. He'll never know whether Martin is one of those self-starters he claims to place such high value on, either, because the public squelching has left the man so angry and hurt that he won't risk presenting an idea again.

This really *is* a waste of time and resources, and it's a classic example of communication breakdown caused by a failure to listen.

THE CRITICAL IMPORTANCE
OF LISTENING

When I am called in to help with communication breakdowns, the first potential problem I check for is a failure to listen. We are such busy people these days! People tell me that they don't have *time* to listen. People who feel uneasy if they're only doing one thing at a time tell me they're willing to listen, but "with only one ear"; their routine practice is to write or read or at minimum think of other things while they are allegedly listening. And there are very honest people who look me right in the eye and say things like these:

"I don't listen because I'm not interested in what other people have to say."

"I don't listen because other people are boring."

"Nothing anybody else might be saying is valuable enough to be worth my time. I give them maybe a couple of seconds."

These statements represent a serious error of judgment. This is how you become someone whose spouse has just walked out for good—and whose child has just run away, or whose entire staff has just resigned—and whose immediate response is, "I didn't even know there was anything wrong!" This is how people find themselves fired "without warning." *Listening is obligatory.*

How We Listen

People tend to think that when they listen they "extract" the speaker's meaning first from the words, and then from the sentences, and then from the complete utterances. But that's just as impossible for human beings as running eighty miles an hour would be. If you really had to do that, in the space of just an average sentence or two you'd be hopelessly behind and you'd never catch up.

Your brain knows better. What really happens when you listen is that you generate utterances of your own right along with the speaker, based on what you already know about him or her and about your language and the situation. Your brain, scanning only for mismatch, can keep up with the stream of language coming at you. Only when the sequence you're generating turns out *not* to match the speaker's do you stop and focus on individual words, and we have special ways of dealing with that event. We say, "Wait a minute! What did you say?" Meaning "What I just heard you say was nothing like what I was saying along with you in my head—I must have misunderstood you. Say it again, please."

This listening process is on automatic for your native language *as long as you don't interfere with it.* But we *do* interfere with it—that's the problem. Your brain can't generate two different sequences of language at the same time, no matter how skilled you are as a communicator; it's impossible. That means that if, as you "listen," you're talking to yourself . . .

I'll bet my parking meter is expired; it's got to be. I know it was at least three o'clock when I parked because I had just talked to Carla and she doesn't get there till three. If I get another ticket . . .

. . . you cannot possibly be listening. The same thing holds if you are rehearsing what you're going to say when *you* get a turn, or thinking how much better you could present what the speaker is trying to present, or wondering if the speaker will *ever* shut up, or planning what you'll have for dinner. All such activities require you to generate sentences that you say to yourself, and there's no way you can listen at the same time. You can *hear*, but you can't listen.

Whether you "don't listen" in the deliberate and open fashion demonstrated by the impatient boss in Scenario B, or, more courteously, you pretend to be listening while you think about something else, the result is the same: You end up with insufficient information on which to base your response, and you do what's called "leaping to conclusions." Carl Heyward leaped to the conclusion—the entirely incorrect conclusion—that Martin Blake had brought in a proposal thrown together in haste as a way of showing off, and his behavior toward Martin was then based on that error. The result was at the least the loss of future input from an employee whose ideas might well have been extremely valuable, perhaps the loss of the solution to an urgent current problem, and most certainly the loss of Martin Blake's trust and good will. All for lack of the simple, but crucial, act of active listening.

The question is, how do you learn to listen effectively? There's no button you can push. How do you proceed? You begin with Miller's Law.

MILLER'S LAW

Psychologist George Miller said it best, in the statement that I call Miller's Law:

> In order to understand what another person is saying, you must assume that it is true and try to imagine what it might be true of. (George Miller, in Hall, 1980)

That is, when someone says to you, "My toaster has been talking to me," the proper response is not the hostile and disagreeable "Listen, I don't have <u>time</u> for stupid jokes!" but "What has it been saying?" And then you pay attention to what comes next.

Everywhere I go, what I see and hear is people applying Miller's Law-In-Reverse. They hear something that strikes them as unacceptable or outrageous; they immediately assume that it's *false*; and they try to imagine what's wrong with the person who said it that would account for their doing so. Remember that listening stops the instant someone starts talking to himself or herself silently, as in *That's the most ridiculous thing I ever heard! Now why is he (she) saying that? I'll bet it's because* . . . You can fill in the blank. *Because he didn't do his homework. Because she'll do anything to get my goat. Because he just doesn't understand this business. Because I can't afford a fancy car like she's driving. Because I'm a woman.* And so on. All of it based on little or no evidence at all.

I don't for one moment believe that most of us do this because we're convinced that it's best always to assume the worst about others. Rather, we do it because we are convinced that if we listen—really listen, with our full attention—it will take too much of our time.

That's unfortunate, because it's almost never true. Usually the person's speaking time isn't nearly as long as we think it is, for one thing. For another, the misunderstandings that come from *not* listening—whether they occur in a business or school situation or in our private lives—usually take much longer to straighten out than listening to the original utterance would have taken. *It's far more efficient to listen.*

DISTORTED PERCEPTIONS OF TIME

We need to spend a little of *our* time examining this phenomenon, because we so consistently use distorted time perceptions as a *reason* for not listening. American doctors—more than 70 percent of whose malpractice suits are for things they said or failed to say, rather than for their actions—are our best example.

Let's make the reasonable assumption that when doctors are allowing patients to talk they are actually listening to them. In a 1984 study, researchers Howard Beckman and Richard Frankel found that the average time doctors allowed patients to talk without interruption was *18 seconds.* The study is particularly interesting because the doctors had agreed to be recorded and knew that the information would be analyzed and written up for a medical journal. We can reasonably conclude, therefore, that the 18-second period they spent in the role of listener was their attempt to demonstrate their *best* listening behavior.

When the doctors were presented with the results of the research, two things happened. First: They insisted that they had let the patients talk for *much* longer than 18 seconds. Second: When the evidence made it clear that they were wrong about that, they explained that they had had a good reason. If they listened to patients without interrupting them they would never get anything done, they told the researchers—because the patients would *talk on and on, endlessly.* Beckman and Frankel did a follow-up study to find out whether that was true. They found that when patients were allowed to talk as long as they wanted, without interruption from the doctors, no patient talked longer than 90 seconds and most talked for only about 30 seconds.

When I tell doctors this in seminars they say, "That may be true of those people, but it's not true in my practice!" And then we try a small experiment of our own. I tell them I'll track the time by the second hand on my watch, and that I want them to yell "Now!" when they think that one minute has gone by. The results are surprising: The "nows" start at about twenty seconds, and sometimes even sooner. No question about it—doctors perceive both themselves and patients talking for a much longer period of time than is actually the case, and this serves as their justification for "I don't have time to listen." But the handful of minutes they save in this way over the course of a day is *no* time compared with the many hours they spend dealing with potential and actual malpractice suits caused by communication breakdowns.

The same thing is happening to all of us. Parents and teachers claim that they don't have time to listen to kids "go on and on about nothing," and take the same attitude toward relatives and friends. Professionals in every field claim that they can't possibly find time to listen to clients and colleagues and customers. The only people who seem willing to listen are couples newly fallen in love, and the therapists we *pay* to listen, at a hundred dollars an hour for the service.

The results are absolutely predictable: Communication breakdowns, followed by personal and workplace crises, often happening "without warning." Dealing with the crises then requires far more of our time than would have been needed if we had just listened—really listened, with our full attention—in the first place.

Finally, it's important to know that there is a bonus for real listening (also called "active listening" and "attending"). The research of James Lynch has proved that real listening is good for your health.

It relaxes you; it improves your blood pressure and heart rate and the flow of all the chemicals that go *with* improved blood pressure and heart rate. It produces a relaxation response. That can't happen if you're interfering with your listening process by maintaining an incessant competing stream of self-talk. It *will* happen, automatically, if you give your attention to the speaker and let your listening brain do its job as it was intended to do.

LEARNING THE SKILL OF ACTIVE LISTENING

For many people, a deliberate effort to apply Miller's Law is enough to trigger active listening. You hear what someone says; you assume—not accept, just assume—that it's true; and you make finding out what it's true *of* your goal. In order to reach that goal you need information, which you can only get by listening. For example . . .

DOCTOR: "Mrs. Smith, I see you're here about chest pain. Now, where is this pain, when does it start, and how long does it last?"

PATIENT: "Doctor, I know what it is. My Aunt Grace had the same thing exactly."

DOCTOR: "Ma'am, I'm not interested in your Aunt Grace. I need information about you. Now—where is your pain, when does it start, and how long does it last?"

Numerous repetitions, with Mrs. Smith insisting that she knows what's wrong and doesn't need to answer all those questions, and the doctor disagreeing . . . winding up with . . .

DOCTOR: "Mrs. Smith, do you want me to help you or NOT? If you expect me to do ANYthing for you, you are going to HAVE to coOPerate!"

PATIENT: "Now YOU LISTEN TO ME, young man! I may be OLD, but I am NOT SEnile!"

This is hostile language on both sides, and it uses up large amounts of time without accomplishing anything useful. Suppose that the doctor instead applies Miller's Law, assumes that Mrs. Smith's statement is true, and investigates that possibility. This is what happens . . .

DOCTOR: "Tell me, Mrs. Smith, when your Aunt Grace had this pain, where was it? When did it start and how long did it last?"

The doctor then listens, the patient provides the information the doctor needs, the interview moves along quickly to a successful conclusion—and there is no hostile language. Mrs. Smith can be relied on to point out any important discrepancy—"When my Aunt Grace had it, it usually came on in the evening, but my pain usually happens around noon." Crucially for a society that lives by the metaphor TIME IS MONEY, money is saved.

When you are convinced that your teenage son is responsible for the dent in your fender and he insists that his sister did it, apply Miller's Law. Begin with, "All right. Tell me, when Janet put the dent in that fender, where was she?" and follow that line, listening to what your son says. If his claim is false, you'll find it out as you go along. If it's true, you will have avoided the fight that goes with saying, "Oh, DON'T give me that! YOU did it, and we both KNOW that, and trying to blame it on your SISter only makes it WORSE!"

But trying to deliberately apply Miller's Law may not be enough. Some people tell me that even when they start a language interaction with a Miller's Law opening, they still can't manage to listen, and the fights happen anyway. The solution for this problem is to practice with your television set, which can't get its feelings hurt, can't get angry, and is at your beck and call. Here's what you do:

1. Find a program where one or more people are talking, using real language—a lecture, a speech, a sermon, something of that kind.

It not only doesn't matter if the speaker is boring, it's *better*. The more boring the experience is, the greater the challenge and the more you'll learn.

2. Set a timer to go off in five minutes, so that you don't have to keep track of the time yourself.

3. Sit down and give your full attention to the speaker.

This means keeping your eyes and ears and thoughts and feelings tuned to the person who's talking. Don't read, don't doodle, don't wonder how you're doing. Concentrate on the stream of speech coming at you.

4. Every time you notice that your attention has wandered—because you have no idea what's just been said, or you realize that you're thinking about something else entirely—grab your attention and return it to the speaker.

When you can deliberately listen to a speaker for five minutes without your attention wandering even once, you've graduated: You're ready to begin listening to real people, face to face. Most of the time you'll find that they won't need the whole five-minute span that you are now capable of giving them.

SHE SAYS/HE SAYS

Listening is one of many aspects of language and communication for which opinions and information usually reflect stereotypes rather than reality. There *is* evidence that women have slightly better hearing than men do, especially in old age, but no evidence that this physiological fact correlates with listening in any significant way. Some people who have difficulty hearing stop trying to listen; others try to compensate for the problem by listening more carefully. The differences are individual rather than by gender. And for both genders it appears that the decision to listen to someone depends not on gender but on two other factors: how interested the listener is in the topic, and the amount of power the speaker has over the listener.

The common stereotype is not so gender-neutral, however: The claim is that men don't listen, and especially that men don't listen to women. As in this example dialogue . . .

SHE: "Honey, I don't see how I'm going to pick a candidate to vote for this time—I don't like <u>any</u> of them! What do <u>you</u> think?"

HE: "Is this the only hot sauce we've got? I thought we had some of that new stuff someplace . . ."

SHE: "The 'new stuff' is right there by your elbow. Did you hear what I said?"

HE: "Sure. But this isn't the one your dad said was so much better, this is that <u>generic</u> stuff! Why didn't you get the other kind?"

SHE: (Sighs) "Sorry. . . . I'll get some."

Certainly there are men who have this listening style, both with women and with other men. But women are just as capable of it as men are, based again on interest and power. For example:

CHILD: "Mom, I can't figure out why Leanne doesn't like me. I like <u>her</u>, and I've never done anything to make her not like me. Do you think she's ever going to like me?"

MOTHER: "<u>Why</u> are you wearing your good sweater on a school day?"

CHILD: "Mom, did you hear what I said?"

MOTHER: "I've told you a hundred times, that sweater is <u>not</u> for school, it's for dress-up!"

CHILD: (Sigh) "Yes, Mom. I'll go put on the other one."

This is not a matter of gender, but of power. Listening is a courtesy that one person offers to another. People who routinely behave like the non-listeners in these two dialogues, whatever their gender, are unwilling to extend that courtesy to someone they perceive as boring and/or having no power to *compel* them to listen. It's a dangerous attitude that tends to become a habit, and it's frequently the explanation for fights—and worse—that come as a complete surprise.

ANOTHER LOOK AT SCENARIO B

What if Carl Hayward had been willing to use Miller's Law in his interaction with Martin Blake? How might things have turned out?

CARL: "Let's hear what you have in mind."

MARTIN: "It's simple, and it's the obvious right move. All we need is a newsletter for the customers in the suburbs that would focus their attention on what a great relationship they have with us."

CARL: [*Of all the dumb ideas! But let's just assume it's true and see what happens.*] "All right. . . . go on."

MARTIN: "I have a stack of studies here proving that for every dollar you put into a newsletter like that you get three dollars back. And I've found a firm that provides <u>generic</u> newsletters, already on the computer, so that all we have to do is drop in a personal paragraph here and there and print the sucker <u>out</u>. I've got all the figures ready—I can explain exactly what it would cost and how it would pay off."

CARL: "Tell you what. . . . Get copies made of all that information, so everybody can take a look at it over the weekend, and then let's talk about it again on Wednesday. Fair enough?"

MARTIN: "Fair enough."

Carl may still end up feeling that Martin's idea is a poor one. But there are very significant differences between this situation and the one shown in the original scenario.

1. Carl will be basing his decision on solid information instead of making it off the top of his head.

2. Carl will see the evidence that Martin worked hard to prepare the proposal.

3. If the idea turns out to be a good one, a problem will have been solved; if it doesn't, the relationship between Carl and Martin will still be one of mutual respect, and Martin won't hesitate to bring forward other ideas in the future.

4. If Carl has to tell Martin that his idea is being rejected, Martin will know that the decision was made after careful and courteous consideration, not in the arrogant and arbitrary way it was done in the original scenario.

5. Whether the final message from Carl to Martin is a positive or negative one, the outcome is much better, for a very small investment of additional time—and there is no loss of face for anyone involved.

Without good listening, there's really no hope of getting rid of hostile language. The payoffs are so substantial that it's worth making the minor effort that mastering this indispensable skill requires.

5

METAPHORS

Scenario C

By the time Tom and Ann left the meeting, Tom knew—from the way she looked and the way she rushed to beat him through the doors—that Ann was furious, but he didn't know why. As soon as they were in the car and on the way back to the office he demanded an explanation.

"You know very <u>well</u> what I'm mad about!," she said, and Tom winced—he could almost see smoke coming out of her ears. "I'm MAD because you LIED in there!"

"I lied?" Now he was *really* baffled. "When?"

"When? When you sat right there and claimed that we already had approval from Ammex on the supply prices, Tom! That's not <u>true</u>, and you know it as well as <u>I</u> do!"

"But <u>wait</u> a minute, Ann . . . I talked to Ammex yesterday and Chet promised me we'd have the papers Friday. I <u>told</u> you about that!"

"That doesn't change one single thing, Tom; that's not what you <u>said</u>. <u>You</u> said we have approval, and <u>that's</u> a LIE!"

"Hey, we got the contract, didn't we?," Tom protested. "That's jobs for twenty people <u>plus</u>, you know! Isn't that what matters here?"

"There's a name for getting a contract that way, Tom," she said bitterly. "It's called <u>fraud</u>."

Tom punched the steering wheel with his fist; he was angry now, too. "I did <u>not</u> <u>lie</u>!"

"What you said wasn't <u>true</u>!"

"Okay, it wasn't true, but it wasn't a <u>lie</u>!"

Ann stared at him. "YOU have no morals at ALL!"

"That's better than being like YOU, Goody Two-Shoes," Tom yelled, "and having no BRAINS!"

WHAT'S GOING ON HERE?

This confrontation is a typical example of one of the most common disagreements English-speaking men and women have in our society. It's like the argument I once had with my department chairman, whose closing line was "Okay, what I said wasn't <u>true</u>, I <u>know</u> that! But it wasn't a <u>lie</u>! Not in <u>that</u> situation!" It's like the common argument husbands and wives have on the way home from class reunions where the woman has listened in astonishment to the version of their lives that the man presented to their former classmates. It's a rare couple that can't remember similar examples.

POINTS OF VIEW

The way Tom perceives the situation, he has done exactly what he should have done, and done it well; it seems to him that he should be getting congratulations from his colleague instead of criticism. He knew it would be hard to land the new contract without price approval for the basic supplies—that's why he knocked himself out the previous day to make sure it would be arriving. He knows and trusts Chet Clayton, the man in charge of these matters at Ammex. When Chet said they'd have the papers in hand by Friday, Tom felt perfectly safe going ahead on that basis. The new contract is important, and it would let them hire a bunch of new people; the idea of putting it at risk over a minor delay strikes him as insane, and as solid evidence that Ann doesn't belong on any negotiating team.

*****

Ann sees matters very differently. She has to sit in a meeting while her colleague presented as final something that she knew was still tentative. She then had to choose between appearing to go along with the misrepresentation—making her a party to the fraud—or calling him on it then and there, which would have meant losing the contract. In Ann's book that's not a choice, that's blackmail, and she bitterly resents being put in such a position. The idea that Tom would lie about something so important—and that he didn't hesitate to drag her down with him—strikes Ann as completely immoral, and as proof that he can't be trusted as a negotiator.

*****

The perceptions Ann and Tom have of what's happened are very different, and very ugly. But in fact this dispute has nothing to do with Tom's morals or Ann's sanity. It's a classic clash over *metaphors*—in two ways.

First: Tom, like the majority of adult American males, operates on the basis of the metaphor LIFE IS A FOOTBALL GAME; Ann, like the majority of adult American women, gives that slot to LIFE IS A TRADITIONAL SCHOOLROOM. The two metaphors are so different that Ann and Tom, even when both observe the same event at the same time and in the same place, often have radically different understandings of what happened and why. These two people are both moral, both intelligent, and both sane, and they agree that lying is immoral. The problem is that they disagree about what *counts* as a lie.

On the football field it's perfectly okay to pretend you have the ball when you don't have it, or to pretend you're going to run one direction and then run the other way. That's not lying, it's just "the way the game is played." It's not only okay, it's admired and rewarded. (The same thing is true, with obvious variations, for other team sports that may serve as metaphors, such as cricket and basketball and soccer.) In the traditional schoolroom, on the other hand, if a statement is false it's a lie. Period; end of discussion. You not only don't get rewarded for lying, you get punished. Tom is basing his decisions on the rules of football, while Ann is basing hers on the rules of the schoolroom; this makes disagreement and hostility almost inevitable.

Second: Both Ann and Tom see their disagreement as a contest in which one person has to be right and the other person has to be wrong. This reflects yet another common metaphor (one that we will explore in detail below): DISAGREEMENT IS COMBAT. The combination of these two metaphorical frames for their behavior creates tension and confusion and an emotional reaction far out of proportion to the seriousness of what has just happened.

WHY METAPHORS MATTER

The word "metaphor" may bring to your mind only classroom experiences in which you tried to remember its definition for a test or struggled to "spot the metaphors" in some writer's prose or poetry.

We all recognize TIME IS MONEY and LIFE IS A BOWL OF CHERRIES as metaphors; we recognize "Cinnamon is a spice" and "Two and two are four" as not metaphors but statements of fact. And we all recognize the difference between these two kinds of language. But our tendency is to believe that facts are important, while metaphors are "only figures of speech" and have nothing much to do with life in the real world.

The truth is that we human beings actually live our lives by and through metaphors, and that metaphors permeate everything we say and do, even in our most intimate moments. *The importance of the metaphors we select to filter our perceptions and organize our experience truly cannot be overestimated.*

At every moment we have to make decisions about what we will do and say next. We almost never have time to sit down and carefully list all the various possibilities, with the reasons for and against each one, before making our choice. Human behavior isn't random and is rarely dictated by instinct; we constantly have to *choose* our next move, very quickly, and usually while doing other things at the same time. A certain percentage of those choices are based on actual rules—*"Don't eat your peas with a spoon"* ... *"No parking"* ... *"Honor thy father and thy mother"*—but the vast majority are made on the basis of our metaphors.

This is tremendously important to understanding the use of hostile language, because *when you choose a metaphor you are also choosing its rules, along with the roles and scripts that those rules dictate.*

As long as men rely on the football metaphor and women rely on the schoolroom metaphor, they'll find themselves in arguments like the one in Scenario C. But if you asked Ann *why* she's insisting that Tom lied, she wouldn't say, "Because the rule in the traditional schoolroom is that any false statement is a lie, and the schoolroom rules are the ones I base my behavior on." Nor would Tom, if asked to explain why he's protesting against Ann's accusation, say that it's because he operates by the rules of football.

We ought to be made aware of this problem as small children, but that doesn't happen. Like fish who are unaware of the water they swim in, we are almost never consciously aware of the metaphors that we're using. This is not a good situation. Metaphors are not trivial. Our lives revolve around them; we need to become consciously aware of them and of their power.

Keeping all this in mind, let's turn to the question of the metaphor we use for *disagreements*.

WHAT IS DISAGREEMENT?

The communication metaphors most commonly chosen in our society today for even the most trivial disagreements are these three, with the majority of people choosing the third:

- DISAGREEMENT IS A CONTEST.

- DISAGREEMENT IS A SPORT.

- DISAGREEMENT IS COMBAT.

For any of those metaphors it would be an error to say, "Oh, that's only a figure of speech!" All three have *competition* as their major component; the third proposes the kind of competition that can end in grave disability or death. In our inner cities today, where you can be knifed or shot for "dissing" someone (that is, speaking to them in a way they consider disrespectful), there is nothing "figurative" about that risk. And the evidence for the health hazards of exposure to hostile language demonstrates that the danger is real even for those of us fortunate enough to live and work in peaceful places. All three metaphors carry with them this rule:

Every disagreement has to end with a winner and a loser.

The difference is only in degree. We can therefore take DIS-AGREEMENT IS COMBAT (often worded as ARGUMENT IS WAR) as the cover metaphor; the roles it contains are The Winner, The Loser, and The Coward Who Runs Away. And the consequences of our culture's choice in metaphors can be clearly seen in the epidemic of hostile and hateful language we're struggling with today. As George Lakoff and Mark Johnson point out:

It is important to see that we don't just talk about arguments in terms of war. . . . Though there is no physical battle, there is a verbal battle, and the structure of an argument—attack, defense, counterattack, etc.—reflects this. It is in this sense that the ARGUMENT IS WAR metaphor is one that we live by in this culture; it structures the actions we perform in arguing. (*Metaphors We Live By*, Lakoff & Johnson, p. 4)

I once complimented an aunt of mine on a handsome piece of stoneware sitting on her mantel by telling her what a beautiful stoneware crock I thought it was. Which brought on:

HER: "That's not a crock. It's a jar."

ME: "Oh . . . I'm sorry. I call them crocks."

HER: "But it's a jar, dear."

ME: "I see. In my dialect it's a crock, but in yours it's a jar. That's interesting, isn't it?"

HER: "Dialects have nothing to DO with it! You're just WRONG when you say it's a crock!"

ME: "All right—I understand."

HER: "You understand what?"

ME: "I understand that you want me to call that piece of stoneware a jar, and I will."

HER: "No, you don't understand at ALL! It's NOT a crock! It's a JAR!"

This didn't end it; I'm sure you could write the rest of the lines yourself, from your personal experience in similar language interactions. It was *ridiculous*, from start to finish.

My aunt was so furious that she was crying, and to this day she remembers (and reminds me of) this argument. A trivial example? No—because it teaches us a crucial lesson about the way our culture perceives and handles disagreements.

It wasn't enough for me to agree to call the stoneware what she called it, which, for politeness's sake, I was more than willing to do. That wouldn't have constituted *victory*, you see. She wanted me to say straight out, with sincerity in my voice, "You're right! It's <u>wrong</u> to call it a crock! I'll never make that mistake again, because now I know that it's wrong. Thank you for setting me straight." We reached a point at which I was so desperate to end the dispute that I *did* say that, but—because I have no acting talent at all—it didn't help. My body language gave me away, and I only made her angrier still. She said, "You're only saying that to shut me UP! You don't MEAN it!" And that was true.

That's still not the end. I've talked to many people about this particular example (one that strikes me as the absolute peak of absurdity) and I am *amazed* at how many respond by trying to start an argument of their own. Not because they care whether the stoneware is called a jar or a crock, but because they insist that I should have "stuck to my guns"—the language of combat—and *refused* to call it a jar. As they see it, I accepted the role of The Coward Who Runs Away, and they disapprove of that in the strongest terms. And they, like my aunt, appear willing to go on arguing about this matter until they can get me to say that they are right and I am wrong—with sincerity in my voice.

In the cold light of day, it's hard to imagine any of these people wasting their time and energy and passion this way. My aunt is a sophisticated and intelligent woman; intellectually, she understands that whether I call her stoneware a jar or a crock is irrelevant. She understands that if I called it a *chair* it would be a serious matter requiring expert attention. She understands the difference between something dangerous—say, my calling the accelerator in my car "the brake"—and the incident I've described. Nevertheless, her whole day was ruined by our disagreement. The people who want to argue with me about how I handled the situation are equally capable of making these distinctions. Why, then, are fights like these so much a staple of our lives? Why do they keep happening?

Because of the power of the metaphor, that's why! All these otherwise rational people have chosen the metaphor that equates verbal conflicts and wars, with its rule that every disagreement must end with a clear winner and a clear loser. When a disagreement comes their way, the combat metaphor includes that rule and they follow it, no matter how ridiculous it is.

This will remind you of the way people stop their cars for a red light even when it's obvious that there are no other cars for many miles. It's the rule, and we are a rule-obeying species. However, we're *conscious* of the rule about red lights; we're aware that that's why we've stopped, and we make a conscious decision to do so. The situation with rules that come from metaphors is different.

DOES OUR CHOICE MAKE SENSE?

The question we have to ask ourselves is: Have we chosen the right metaphor for disagreement? Does its obligatory winner/loser rule make sense in our lives? Obviously, we're *fond* of it, and we feel comfortable with it the way we feel comfortable in a favorite chair. But can we defend it? We can logically say that unless we *always* stop for a red light we might forget to stop when our lives depend on it. If we could show that the winner/loser rule for arguments is like that, there'd be justification for following it.

We can't do it. We can produce real world evidence that following the "Stop for every red light" rule actually saves lives and prevents injuries and property damage on a huge scale. We have no such evidence for the value of the winner/loser rule in disagreements. It's possible to force other people to say what we want them to say; it's not possible to force them to *mean* it. And we have much evidence that trying to change someone's mind by verbal force wastes our time and energy and can literally destroy human relationships. Unless and until that changes, treating disagreement as combat is a serious communication error.

Giving up errors of this kind isn't simple, however. Arguing about "a stoneware jar" versus "a stoneware crock" is absurd. But consider what happens when exactly the same *type* of disagreement, the same language pattern, is about a less trivial subject, as in these examples.

Talking about hunting deer:

"It's not a harvest, it's a <u>slaughter</u>!"

Talking about abortion:

"It's not a therapeutic procedure, it's <u>mur</u>der!"

Talking about spiritual matters:

"It's not a religion, it's a <u>cult</u>!"

Talking about military matters:

"It's not a police action, it's a <u>war</u>!"

Talking about sexual preferences:

"It's not a lifestyle, it's an <u>abomina</u>tion!"

These examples demonstrate very clearly what's really going on. As with the red light rule, people behave as if they must follow the winner/loser rule for *every* disagreement because they might otherwise fail to do so when it really matters. But unlike the red light rule, it isn't a conscious decision, something they deliberately plan to do and work at doing; on the contrary; it's outside conscious awareness.

When you talk to people who've found themselves in the middle of ferocious arguments over things they freely admit they don't even care about, they say things like this: "I don't know <u>why</u> I kept on arguing—it didn't matter to me at all! But I felt like I <u>had</u> to—I mean, I couldn't just back down and give <u>up</u>!" They don't realize that this feeling of obligation is based on the DISAGREEMENT IS COMBAT metaphor. In combat it's a disgrace to "just back down and give up"; when you argue by the rules of the battlefield, you lock yourself into battlefield standards of conduct.

The hazard is that when we deal with a part of our behavior for which our reasons are outside our conscious awareness, we have a strong tendency to describe that behavior as "natural and right," as "self-evident," as "just the way things are," or even "the only <u>possible</u> way things could be." For example, here is Gerry Spence, on page 197 of *How To Argue and Win Every Time*:

"I am speaking of a simple mind-set. The mind-set does not make room for loss. The mind-set is one that extends permission, but only to win."

Spence (like many others who take the position that winning is everything) claims here that agreeing to disagree—saying "Okay, I think it's a crock and you think it's a jar, and that's all right, because we both know what we're talking about"—is dishonorable and out of the question. But in fact there is nothing self-evident about DIS-AGREEMENT IS COMBAT, nor is there any moral code that commands us to choose and maintain it as our metaphor. *Human beings are free to choose a different metaphor, with different rules.*

Hostile language is becoming the norm in our society because we've made the mistake of treating DISAGREEMENT IS COMBAT as if it were a statement of *fact*. We don't have any choice about statements of fact. We can't decide to say, "Two and two are six" and base our behavior on that statement—it won't work, and it will cause us endless and intolerable trouble in the real world. Metaphors are different. It's certainly true that we are under tremendous pressure from others to accept the metaphors they have chosen; our media, in particular, constantly drum consensus metaphors into us. But that doesn't make them *facts*. We are free to say, "I reject that metaphor" and look for a new one. We need a metaphor for disagreement that makes it acceptable and honorable for people to reason together, so that we can begin following its rules instead of the rules of combat.

In *Metaphors We Live By*, Lakoff and Johnson (1980) write:

> "Try to imagine a culture where arguments are not viewed in terms of war, where no one wins or loses . . . Imagine a culture where an argument is viewed as a dance, the participants are seen as performers, and the goal is to perform in a balanced and aesthetically pleasing way." (pp. 4–5)

They conclude that our culture would probably insist that people involved in such a process weren't arguing at all—that they were doing some quite different thing. I agree. The distance between DIS-AGREEMENT IS COMBAT and DISAGREEMENT IS DANCE is so vast that we can't make the mental leap required. It would be like trying to understand and accept A ROSE IS A CAST IRON SKIL-LET—it makes no sense to us. However, that doesn't mean we have to accept the combat metaphor.

Suppose you and I are building a bookcase or a barn together. Unless we are pathologically competitive, we'll do that by cooperating to get the job done, and we'll consider winning and losing *irrelevant* to what we're doing. Only habit and inertia and unawareness keep us from looking upon disagreement as an occasion for building a mutual understanding that can serve as a foundation for future interaction, instead of as a fight to the death.

If disagreement is combat, the only goal that those who disagree have in common is that of establishing who wins and who loses. If disagreement is carpentry, on the other hand, their shared goal is to build—together—a conclusion that both can live with, even if that conclusion goes no farther than "We can agree to disagree."

COMBAT VERSUS CARPENTRY

Let's look for just a moment at the language of these two semantic fields to see how they fit our needs. I'll first offer a typical combat utterance, and then a "translation" into the language of carpentry . . .

1. "My strategy in a disagreement is to get in there at the very beginning and attack."

   "My strategy in a disagreement is to lay a careful foundation at the very beginning."

2. "He shot down every one of her arguments."

   "He took apart every one of her arguments."

3. "This is a battle over <u>principles</u>, not just opinions."

   "This discussion is built on <u>principles</u>, not just opinions."

4. "Logic is not our most useful weapon in a disagreement."

   "Logic is not our most useful tool in a disagreement."

5. "You can't let down your guard with him around, not even for a minute."

   "You can't lay down your tools with him around, not even for a minute."

6. "That first argument was a real bombshell—it just tore our case apart."

"That first argument was like a thunderstorm—it stopped us from building our case."

7. "It's easy to shoot holes in her arguments."

   "It's easy to find the weak places in her arguments."

8. "Every word he said was meant to cut like a knife."

   "Every word he said was meant to cause serious damage."

9. "I protected myself by using accurate facts and figures as a shield."

   "I made sure my case would hold together by using accurate facts and figures."

10. "He came charging in with statistics that cut our arguments to pieces."

    "He started hammering his case down with statistics that pointed out every weak plank in our arguments."

11. "You can't mount a successful attack if you're afraid to speak up."

    "You can't construct a successful case if you're afraid to speak up."

As you can immediately see, it's no more complicated or difficult (and no less true to English) to use the vocabulary of carpentry to talk about disagreement than it is to use the vocabulary of war. All of the same necessary messages are being transmitted; what's left out are the messages of *hostility*. This really is a matter of choice, not of necessity.

THE LAST PIECE OF THE PUZZLE—THE DOCTRINE OF THE JUST WAR

A human culture is a patchwork quilt, with lots of different pieces. One of the most central blocks of our cultural quilt is the doctrine of *The Just War*. We grow up on its principles; we make countless moral decisions, large and small, on that basis. Our problem with war is that another piece of the quilt has embroidered on it the words "Thou shalt not kill." Society has had to figure out how you bring people up to obey *that* rule while at the same time maintaining the armies necessary for national defense. You can't expect men and women who feel guilt and shame about killing to be—or to raise—good soldiers.

The doctrine of the Just War offers us an ingenious solution to this contradiction. It doesn't say "Killing in combat isn't <u>real</u> killing, so you're not breaking the rules." It doesn't say "Killing in combat is <u>okay</u>, so you're not breaking the rules." Instead, it says that when people die as a result of actions taken in a just war the killing is nothing more than an *unfortunate and unavoidable side effect* of those actions. That is: In combat your intent is not to kill but to carry out the honorable defense of your home and country. *Therefore*, what you're doing is not only moral but admirable.

Our DISAGREEMENT IS COMBAT metaphor includes the idea that the combat must be just, the principle that violence is permissible when it can't be avoided, and the practice of labeling the results of such violence as side effects rather than intended goals. But the doctrine of the Just War has one *more* important principle, one that is the very heart of what "unavoidable" is supposed to mean:

A war can be considered just if and only if *every other way of dealing with the problem has been tried without success* and war is the only alternative that remains.

In our language interactions, that principle has gotten lost. In verbal disagreements, force has gone from last resort, where the just war doctrine can be properly applied, to *first* resort, where it is perverted. Today we have fourteen-year-old boys who have killed other children looking us right in the eye and saying, "Damn right I shot him. I <u>had</u> to!" Followed by the reason they "had to," which turns out to be that the victim "dissed" the killer.

We are very firm advocates of the principle that violent acts are *justified* if they are what you have to do to achieve an accepted goal. Not only justified but often admirable, as we demonstrate by awarding medals or trophies or salaries of millions of dollars a year. By and large we allow only men to *apply* the principle directly (in military combat, for example, or in football and hockey, or in boxing), but we expect our women to support and nurture it so that males will grow up capable of its application. (This is one reason why I call verbal violence "training wheels" for physical violence.) I don't think we could turn this situation around now even if we wanted to. However, there is one thing we *can* do: We can put back into place that part of the metaphor which specifies that violence—in word or in deed—must always be the *last resort*.

In order to do that successfully, however, people have to know that other alternatives—the first, second, and later resorts—exist, and what they *are*! In football we know many things we can do to score touchdowns before we have to resort to brutality. We can run long distances at top speed; we can throw and catch long passes; we can skillfully make it difficult for other players to get in the way of those who are completing the runs and passes. There are similar techniques to use when the field of conflict is not the football field but the field of language interaction—our problem today is that so many people are unaware even that they *exist*.

This is something we *can* fix. We can relearn the techniques that make disagreement without violence possible, and put them into practice in our lives. The information isn't difficult to understand, and the techniques are easy to learn; we just have to have the will to go forward. To achieve that goal we have to do three things:

- Become consciously aware of the DISAGREEMENT IS COMBAT metaphor and its consequences.

- Set that metaphor aside for a new one (like DISAGREEMENT IS CARPENTRY).

- Learn and use the *alternatives* to verbal force.

HE SAYS/SHE SAYS

The clash between the prevailing male metaphor (FOOTBALL) and the corresponding female metaphor (TRADITIONAL SCHOOL-ROOM) leads to arguments about many other key definitions and concepts beside those associated with lying. On the football field, knocking down a member of your own team who happens to be in the way as you run for a touchdown is not BETRAYAL or DISLOY-

ALTY. Working with another player to achieve a goal is not CHEAT-ING. This is totally unlike the schoolroom.

Both the football and the schoolroom metaphors are in operation during disagreements, when the DISAGREEMENT IS COMBAT metaphor kicks in. The results of their combination, as would be expected, are different in the two cases.

On the football field, violence that is an unavoidable side effect of "the way the game is played" is acceptable—it's how you win, and winning is the whole point of football. Football not only permits but encourages shoving other players, falling on them when they're down, and taking the ball away from them against their will. None of these acts is considered violent; they come under the rubric of Things That A Man Has To Do.

In the traditional schoolroom, by contrast, any "physical persuasion" of another pupil is forbidden and punished, especially if you are female. In the schoolroom, if an act involves force and causes pain, it's violence. That's why the issue of whether teachers and principals may spank students has such passionate advocates on both sides of the question. On the football field, it's violence only if it goes beyond the acts permitted by the rules. A football player can't hit another player over the head with a brick, for example—but only because it's "against the rules." Many equally painful and—by schoolroom standards, equally violent—acts are just fine.

So long as this is true, major disagreements between men and women about what constitutes violence will continue. Trying to make a man feel guilty about something he perceives as a necessity, as Ann tries to do in Scenario C, is useless and counterproductive. It only convinces him that he's being treated unjustly and is obligated to defend himself. Trying to make a woman feel obligated to behave according to the rules and ethical principles of football is equally futile.

Suppose you're involved in a disagreement with someone of the opposite sex whom you ordinarily consider rational and intelligent, and suddenly it seems to you that that person has lost his or her mind. If you're a man, stop and ask yourself this question: "What if this were happening in a schoolroom? What would be the rules that apply to the situation?" If you're a woman, ask yourself the same question, but locate it on the football field. If the crux of the argument is a metaphor clash, you will still disagree—but you will be much less likely to feel that the other person is without morals and/or intelligence, because you will understand what's really going on.

Very rarely, it does happen that a man turns out to be using the schoolroom metaphor; I had a client once for whom this was the major problem he faced in communicating both with women and with other men. Even more rarely, a woman turns out to be using the football metaphor, which also guarantees problems. The solution, whatever the genders involved, is the same: Find out what metaphor or metaphors the other person is shaping their behavior by, and work with them with conscious awareness.

ANOTHER LOOK AT SCENARIO C

The communication strategy Tom and Ann should have followed will now be obvious to you and doesn't have to be spelled out in detail. At the moment when Ann explains to Tom why she feels that he lied, Tom needs to explain to her that they're caught in a metaphor clash, just as I've explained it above. He should explain that so far as he is concerned, false statements that do no harm and help you win the game are *not lies*. He should acknowledge that he knows she sees things differently—but point out to her that even in the schoolroom, people are supposed to avoid *brutal* truths. When a homely child says, "Am I really ugly?," adults don't answer with "You sure are. You're the ugliest kid I ever saw." And children who get caught doing that are scolded for it and told to shape up. He and Ann have that much in common where lies are concerned.

Alternatively, Ann can explain to Tom. It makes no difference which one initiates the explanation, as long as they both understand. that what they have to do is agree to disagree. And then some version of the following dialogue must take place:

ANN: "Okay, now I understand what's going on. But we have to negotiate some rules here."

TOM: "Like what?"

ANN: "Like if you're going to do what you did today, you have to warn me ahead of time, so that I have a chance to tell you how

I feel about it and try to change your mind, and so that if you go ahead with it I won't be taken by surprise."

TOM: "That's fair—no problem."

They may want to negotiate a very different arrangement from the one I've just outlined, but they do have to work out the rules, together. Otherwise, their mutual mistrust will guarantee their failure as a negotiating team.

Whenever a disagreement can be traced to a clash between metaphors, get that difference out into the open where it can be explored and worked with.

PART THREE

TECHNIQUES

6

USING THE SATIR MODES

Scenario D

"Well, look at <u>that</u>, will you?" Barbara leaned toward Nora as they headed down the hall toward the copying machine, and nudged her with one sharp elbow. "Unless my eyes are <u>failing</u> me, that is actually Ruth <u>Brown</u>, sitting at her <u>desk</u>!" She jerked her head toward the glass that walled off Ruth's office.

"What?" Nora asked, puzzled. "I mean, why <u>wouldn't</u> she be at her desk?"

Barbara snickered. "<u>Well</u>, Nora," she said, sarcasm dripping from every syllable, "it's only twenty minutes after nine, <u>right</u>? That's very early in<u>deed</u> for Ms. <u>Brown</u> to be making an appearance!"

"Really," Nora said, letting the word trail vaguely off into silence, hoping Barbara would drop the subject—but the other woman was only getting started. She didn't let it interfere with their work; she got the copier running and the task underway without missing a beat. But she went right on talking about Ruth's failings. Ruth had come in after ten o'clock the previous day. Ruth had been late three days out of five last week. So far as Barbara knew, there had *never* been a week when Ruth was on time every single day. It wasn't fair—nobody *else* was allowed to choose their own hours; why should *Ruth* get special treatment?

It went on and on, and Nora grew more and more uncomfortable. She didn't know whether what Barbara was saying was true or not, and she didn't especially care. She just wished Barbara would cut it out.

I <u>hate</u> gossip! Nora thought. *But I have to work with Barbara on this new project every single day for the next six <u>months</u>! What am I going to <u>do</u>?*

Barbara gathered up the stack of copies and piled them on her arm, ready to go back to their desks; she lowered her voice to a confidential near-whisper and spoke near Nora's ear. "You have to wonder," she said, "what Ruth Brown <u>does</u> for the people in charge that makes none of the rules apply to <u>her</u>!"

Nora cleared her throat. "Here," she said briskly, avoiding Barbara's eyes, trying for a smile and knowing it looked anything but real, "let me carry some of those copies! They're <u>way</u> too heavy for one person to carry by herself!"

Barbara's eyebrows went up sharply, and her eyes narrowed. "Oh, don't bother about <u>me</u>!" she said icily. "<u>I'll</u> manage! I always <u>do</u>!" And away she stalked, with her back rigid and her head absurdly high.

WHAT'S GOING ON HERE?

Opinions about gossip—comments made about others who aren't present to clarify the information or defend themselves—vary widely. In the scenario above we have two people who must work together and whose feelings on the subject are at the most extreme opposite ends of the judgment spectrum.

POINTS OF VIEW

Nora has two objections to Barbara's behavior. First, she has no reason to believe that Barbara's statements about Ruth are accurate; second, Nora is opposed to gossip on general principles. But she knows it will be hard to work with Barbara as closely as their schedules require in the coming months if she makes an enemy of her. This puts her in a serious bind. She doesn't want to join in the gossip, and she doesn't want to alienate the other woman. It's clear to her now that she has failed badly in her attempt to balance those two goals. She dreads having to go on working with Barbara.

*****

Barbara enjoys gossip and looks upon it as a perfectly acceptable activity between colleagues and friends. Her resentment of what she sees as special treatment for Ruth Brown is real and intense, and when she finds herself scheduled for a long project with Nora she considers it important—and a sign of friendship—to share that resentment with her and try to persuade Nora to join in. When Nora rejects her overtures, Barbara is embarrassed and hurt; she will be extremely reluctant to treat Nora as a friend again. And she'll look someone to gossip with about her perception that Nora thinks she's better than other people, that Nora likes to put her colleagues down, and so on. She doesn't look forward to having to spend the next six months with someone like that.

This is a classic disagreement of a type you run into every day. The two people involved could just as easily be two men (or a woman and a man), one resentful of the special treatment a third employee appears to be getting from their bosses, the other unwilling to be drawn into the gossip but leary of alienating a colleague. The charges against Ruth Brown are relatively minor, but they could just as easily be charges of serious, even illegal behavior. As was true with the argument in Chapter 5 over whether to call something a crock or a jar, what's important here is not the details, but the *pattern*. This is one of the standard dilemmas with the potential for becoming hostile speech: a situation in which one individual disagrees with another and would like to make the disagreement clear, but is held back from doing so by fear of creating another, perhaps worse, conflict.

Put yourself in Nora's place for a moment. There are two questions you need answers to:

• What—exactly—is your message?

• How can you shape your message so that it will be understood, without making a pleasant future relationship difficult or impossible?

CHOOSING AND SHAPING YOUR NEGATIVE MESSAGE

In every discussion of hostile language, no matter how heated it may become, one area of consensus exists: Everyone involved agrees that life in human societies cannot be carried on without negative messages. It would be useful, therefore, to look at negative messages as a *set* and identify the most frequent and basic types (shown in Figure 1 on page 101). The first cut in sorting negative messages into types is between *bad news*—which is information that should just be reported—and *disagreements*, for which it's appropriate to include judgments and opinions.

Bad News

Figure 1 shows a list of possible messages that report bad news, including the news that someone has died, that someone has a disease, that someone's child has been arrested, that someone's loan application has been rejected, and so on. An infinite number of possible messages of this kind exist, and none of us can know which ones we'll find ourselves speaking or hearing. We can state unequivocally that bad news messages can be eliminated in advance from the equally infinite set of *hostile* messages. There's no need to deliver bad news in hostile language, and no excuse for it. There are always ways to report bad news that will also carry an emotional message which is either neutral or positive.

Suppose I have to tell another person that he or she has done an assigned task incorrectly. I do have to say something like, "You did that incorrectly" or "You made some mistakes when you did that." I do *not* have to say anything like these five examples:

1. "You DID that incorRECTly!"

2. "YOU made some misTAKES when you did THAT!"

3. "Well, you DID IT wrong!"

4. "Well, you really fouled THAT up!"

5. "Can't you do ANYthing RIGHT?"

I may, for personal reasons, have a strong *desire* to deliver the news as in examples 1–5, with all the hostile metamessages added in, but no case can be made that it's *necessary* to do so.

Disagreements

For our purposes, disagreements can be divided into three basic message groups:

- "Your facts are wrong."

- "I object to *X*."

- "Your *X* is/are unacceptable."

(I'm using the word "wrong" here to mean *factual error*, not moral error. Please keep that in mind as we go along.)

1. "Your facts are wrong."

This is the message type you use when someone says the plane is leaving at 6:15 and you have reason to believe that it's leaving at 6:45. Often such disagreements can be easily settled because the facts can be checked and verified. As in delivering bad news, no case can be made for the idea that this requires hostile language. You're saying to the other person, "I hear your statement of the facts; I disagree with that statement." You may or may not also be saying that you're prepared to offer an alternative version of the disputed facts.

2. "I object to/disagree with your claims."

Or your perceptions, your attitude, your behavior, your values, your politics, your religion, etc.—or "I object to you, personally."

3. "Your work is unacceptable."

Or your performance, your results, your plans, your appearance, etc.—or "You, personally, are unacceptable."

These two negatives, types 2 and 3, are similar, but there is an important difference between them.

In type 2 the message is that you have a negative reaction to the other person's claims, perceptions, etc., and that you want to register your objections. Type 2 negative messages mean that "I"—the person speaking—object or disagree. If the message is that someone *else* feels that way and the speaker has been told to pass that information along, the message is then only bad news.

In type 3, the message is that the other person's performance, results, etc., or the individual as a person, are *unacceptable*, which means only that some standard—the speaker's, someone else's, or both—has not been met.

Suppose I'm hiring for my local fire department, and we have a requirement that all firefighters must be at least 5 feet 2 inches tall. Suppose you apply, and you are 5 feet 1 inch tall. When I tell you that you don't meet the department's height standards, I am saying

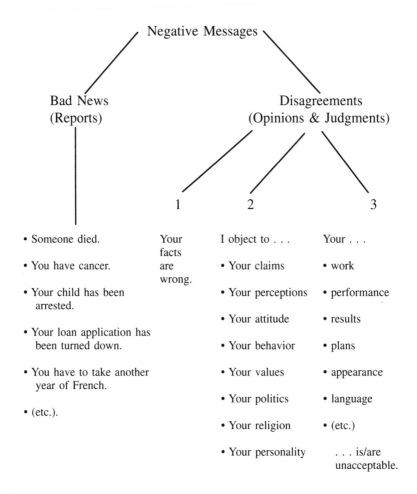

Figure 1

that your height is unacceptable but I am not saying that there's something factually or morally *wrong* with being 5 feet 1 inch. The distinction is an important one, and—as we'll learn later in the book—it's often possible to construct a message of this kind in such a way that it becomes a report of bad news.

Before delivering any negative message, we need to decide which of the groups in Figure 1 it belongs to; only then can we consider whether hostile language is genuinely *required* for what we are about to say.

Consider the situation in Scenario D. We know what Nora's goal is: *She doesn't want to be involved in Barbara's gossip.* Clearly, she needs to deliver a message of disagreement. But here are just seven of the many possible—and very different—such messages to Barbara that Nora might have in mind:

1. *Your facts are wrong.*

   "I disagree with your <u>claims</u>—I don't believe Ruth Brown is late any oftener than anyone else is."

2. *I object to your attitude.*

   "I don't think it's a big deal if Ruth Brown is late all the time. Who cares, as long as she carries her share of the workload?"

3. *I object to your perceptions.*

   "In my opinion, when Ruth Brown comes to work is nobody's business but Ruth Brown's."

4. *Your language is unacceptable to me.*

   "I disapprove of the way you're talking about Ruth Brown."

5. *I object to your behavior.*

   "I disapprove of <u>gossip</u>. It's wrong to talk about people behind their backs when they don't have a chance to defend themselves."

6. *I object to you personally.*

   "I disapprove of <u>you</u>—because you're gossiping about someone, talking about her behind her back."

7. *I object to you personally; what's more, you deserve my contempt.*

   "I don't gossip, and I don't listen to people who <u>do</u>, so you might as well drop it."

Barbara speaks English; she's as aware of the possibilities as Nora is. If Nora makes one or more of the messages explicit by stating it openly, the two women will at least know where they stand. But ducking the issue leaves Barbara free to decide for *herself* which of these messages (or which other member of the set of possibilities) was intended, and her choice may be completely wrong. The same thing will happen if Nora just says, "Please don't" or "Let's talk about something else." That may be fine for two people who rarely see each other and are working together for only a few hours, but it won't do for a long-term working relationship.

Nora's message might have been, "I don't think Ruth Brown is late any oftener than anybody else" or "I disapprove of gossip." But she's left Barbara free to decide that it was "I disapprove of you," or worse, and *that* is the message Barbara will base her behavior toward Nora on in the future. What Nora might have felt or thought is irrelevant if she makes no attempt to get her message across; she has to live with the consequences of Barbara's *guesses* about her thoughts and feelings.

This kind of linguistic gambling is unwise and unnecessary. Before going into any disagreement, take these two preparatory steps:

Step One:

Decide exactly what your message is. Do you disagree with the other speaker's facts, with the emotions being expressed, or both? Do you object to the particular utterance you're hearing, or to the actions or perceptions it represents? Is your disagreement based on principle, on opinion, or something else? Decide *before* you start talking.

Step Two:

Consider the possibility that the message you've chosen could take a positive shape. Look for something on which everyone involved could *agree*, that might serve as the first plank in a negotiated structure everyone could accept and build on.

Is there something like that, something *positive*, that Nora might say to Barbara? Think about it; we'll come back to it later in this chapter when we take another look at Scenario D.

Shaping Your Message With the Satir Modes

One of the most wonderful characteristics of language is its flexibility. For most meanings there are a multitude of possible forms, in terms of both the words used and the body language that goes with them. The problem is that we tend to *behave* as if there were only two ways to choose—by habit and at random. If our usual response to criticism is "I do the best I *can*, you know!" we may rely on that single sentence for every such situation without considering any other possibilities. Or we may rely on our ability to "wing it" and pick something useful from the abundance of possibilities, without any strategy or careful thought.

This is a waste of the potential our language offers. All utterances are not created equal; some are far more likely to achieve the speaker's linguistic goals than others are. What we need are techniques and strategies for reducing the theoretically infinite number of possible shapes for a given meaning (that is, the words and body language that are its spoken form) to a much smaller and more manageable set—plus techniques and strategies for choosing the best alternative from that reduced set. One such technique is the skillful use of the language behavior patterns called Satir Modes.

Virginia Satir was a superb family therapist. In the course of a lifetime of practice, she discovered that when people are trying to communicate under stress their language falls into one of five patterns: Blaming, Placating, Computing, Distracting, and Leveling. We can use these patterns to get past the "by habit or at random" barrier.

You already know the Satir Modes well, although you may not have known their names; they are part of the grammar of English and you use one or more of them constantly. Let's look at a few examples.

Suppose a boss comes out of his office, marches over to an employee's desk, puts his hands on his hips, and yells, "Will you PLEASE explain to me why you aren't through with that report YET?" Here are typical responses from the Satir Modes . . .

Blaming:

- "Because you never give me enough TIME, THAT'S why!"

- "I didn't even GET the darned report till this MORning!"

- "NObody could do this report as fast as YOU want it done!"

- "How do you exPECT me to get it done when you keep YELLing at me?"

Recognize that pattern? It's marked by the use of very personal vocabulary, frequent use of emphatic stresses on words and parts of words, frequent use of words like "always, every, never, nothing, everybody, nobody," and threatening body language. The impression it creates is one of *anger*.

Placating:

- "Oh, am I taking too LONG? I'm so SORry! I'm TRYing to hurry, REALLY I am! Could you give me just a LITTLE more TIME?"

- "I'm slow . . . you KNOW I am! But I always do good WORK!"

- "PLEASE don't yell at me. . . ."

- "I can't beLIEVE you're going to stand there and YELL at me like that when you KNOW how hard I'm TRYing! I just can't be-LIEVE it!"

Like Blaming, Placating relies on lots of personal vocabulary and emphatic stresses on words and parts of words. Unlike Blaming, the impression it creates is one of wimpiness and apology, with body language to match.

Computing:

- "People who want three days work done in three hours are sure to be disappointed."

- "A thirty-page report can't be completed in three hours."

- "When the time allowed for a job isn't long enough, the work doesn't get done."

You will have noticed that both Blaming and Placating have two of the characteristics that identify language as hostile. Computing is different: It avoids personal vocabulary and relies on indefinites and generics and abstractions, and it avoids the use of emphatic stresses. The impression created is one of neutrality and control, both in words and in body language.

Distracting:

Because it contains nothing new, we can skip this one. Distracters cycle through the other modes, with a sentence or two from one, then a sentence or two from another, and the body language shifting to match. This creates an impression only of panic; it's unfortunate, and it's rare.

Leveling:

• "Because three hours isn't enough time to do the job."

• "I'm not through because I need more time."

• "I'll get it finished as soon as I can."

Leveling is what's left over. When you observe the language of someone communicating under stress and you notice that the pattern isn't Blaming, Placating, Computing (or their combination in Distracter Mode), you know that it's Leveling.

We *should* make deliberate strategic choices among the Satir Modes, but we rarely do. No one teaches us to do that, or shows us how. Instead, we tend to have a particular Satir Mode that it's our *habit* to rely on in particular locations or roles in our life. One person always deals with conflict at work by Blaming, for example, but uses Placating in similar situations at home. Another person does it the other way around. Still another, hopelessly at sea, relies on Distracting everywhere except in the most intimate situations, where Leveling seems safe to him or her. We don't ordinarily choose a Satir Mode because we know what it can accomplish and have decided that it's our best choice. Instead, we use the Satir Mode we prefer, usually on the basis of habit alone; often that preference is based on nothing more than what we observed the adults around us doing as we were growing up.

It doesn't have to be like that, and it shouldn't be. We can learn, very quickly, to choose among the Satir Modes for good linguistic reasons, with the avoidance of hostile language as our goal. Let's go back and look at two of the seven possible messages Nora could have given to Barbara (on page 102) to see how the Satir Modes could have been used in each case. Nora has listened to several negative remarks about Ruth Brown, remember, and she wants to object . . .

- *Your facts are wrong.*

  BLAMING: "Listen, that's not TRUE! Why don't you ever check your FACTS before you start making wild CLAIMS about people? I don't want to hear any more ABOUT it!"

  PLACATING: "Oh, I KNOW what you MEAN, and it's AWful the way Ruth takes adVANtage! But you know, I really DON'T think she is late THAT often! And YOU know how I am . . . it upSETS me when people say bad things about others . . . PLEASE stop. . . ."

  COMPUTING: "Many people are unfamiliar with the reasons for others' schedules, and that can lead to misunderstanding. It's not a good idea to base judgments on inadequate information."

  LEVELING: "I don't believe Ruth is late any oftener than anyone else is. I'd appreciate it if you'd stop saying that she is."

- *I object to your behavior.*

  BLAMING: "WHY do you ALWAYS stand around GOSsiping and CRITicizing people? If there's ONE thing I won't put up with, it's GOSsip, and if you want to get along with ME you'll cut it OUT!"

  PLACATING: "You know, I DON'T want to offend you in any way—you KNOW I'm NOT that kind of PERson! But I just feel like I have to TELL you . . . I mean, we have to WORK together, you KNOW? . . . I just feel really unCOMfortable with gossip. I'm SO sorry to seem difficult, but could we please just talk about something ELSE?"

  COMPUTING: "Research shows that gossip causes a great deal of trouble in business situations; the risk is usually greater than the possible benefits."

LEVELING: "Barbara, I don't like gossip; I think it's cruel and underhanded. We'll get along a lot better without it."

The strategy for choosing the best alternatives from these examples—the best ways to disagree without being disagreeable—is obvious. (Distracting, which is panic, was of course eliminated in advance.) The Blaming and Placating versions are hostile and will breed more hostility; the Computing and Leveling versions are the better choices. This gives us our first rule:

Rule One:

> *Avoid Blamer and Placater Mode whenever possible.*

> That is: Avoid the use of personal vocabulary; avoid the use
> of emphatic stresses that signal hostility; avoid the body
> language that goes with Blaming and Placating.

The next question is: How do you decide whether to Compute or to Level?

Leveling is in theory the most perfect communication possible: the plain and simple truth, free of all game-playing and distortion. The other Satir Modes signal a mismatch between the speaker's inner feelings and the language used to express them. People who are afraid they have no power use Blaming in an attempt to create an "I have ALL the power, and I'm not afraid to USE it!" impression. People who care desperately about the approval of others use Placating's "Oh, YOU know me! I don't care! WHATever!" message patterns. Computer Mode's surface message is "I have no emotions; I'm entirely neutral," but the speaker often uses it to *conceal* an emotion. Only with Leveling can you be sure that the speaker's inner feelings and the speaker's words and body language all match.

Theoretically, therefore, Leveling is flawless. But suppose your boss believes that you dislike her, and she's right. Suppose she calls you into her office and says—playing no games, Leveling all the way—"You don't like me, do you?" If you Level right back at her, the dialogue will go like this:

BOSS: "You don't like me, do you?"

YOU: "No, I really don't. I can't stand you, actually."

In the real world, as opposed to the world of theory, that's probably not a good communication strategy. In such a situation, the wise move is to use Computing and say something like this: "As everyone knows, nothing is more mysterious than personal feelings." If the boss is wise, she'll agree and change the subject; if she doesn't, each successive attempt she makes to pin you down should be met with another innocuous platitude, until she is worn out enough to give it up.

If we take the theoretical superiority of Leveling and modify it for use in the real world, the result is our second rule:

Rule Two:

When it's safe and appropriate to do so, Level; otherwise, or if you're not certain what to do, use Computer Mode.

Those two rules will narrow down the millions of possible formats for a message of disagreement and serve as a first step toward constructing such messages skillfully and without using hostile language.

SHE SAYS/HE SAYS

As was the case for listening, the information available about gender behavior and the Satir Modes reflects stereotypes rather than reality. After I have described and demonstrated these patterns in seminars, I always ask for comments and questions. Without exception, someone in my audience says, "Blamers are male and Placaters are female, right?" And it's not unusual for someone to suggest that men do all the Computing and Leveling and that only women use Distracter Mode.

No evidence exists for any of those conclusions. They come directly from the stereotype that all men under stress are strong, masterful, and brutal, while all women under stress are whiny, emotional, and manipulative. In no way do they represent reality.

I have been a close observer of verbal conflicts for all of my adult life. Since the 1960s that observation and work with the resulting data has been my profession. My seminars have never been restricted by gender; the clients in my consulting practice have been about evenly divided between males and females. Because I grew up in a family of trial lawyers, I was given ample opportunity to observe verbal conflict from the cradle on—often more than I would have chosen to have. And I have seen just as many male Placaters as female ones, and just as many female Blamers and Computers and Levelers as male ones. As for Distracters, remember that Distracting reflects panic. Anyone (of any gender) might show that behavior during an acute crisis, but it's virtually unknown for someone to shift to Distracting for every tense or anxious moment.

Now let's go back to Scenario D and rewrite it as it might have gone if Nora had been familiar with the Satir Modes technique.

ANOTHER LOOK AT SCENARIO D

BARBARA: (leaning toward Nora and nudging her with one sharp elbow): "Well, look at <u>that</u>, will you? Unless my eyes are <u>failing</u> me, that is actually Ruth <u>Brown</u>, sitting at her <u>desk</u>!"

NORA: "What? I mean, why <u>wouldn't</u> she be at her desk?"

BARBARA: "<u>Well</u>, it's only twenty minutes after nine, <u>right</u>? That's very early <u>indeed</u> for Ms. <u>Brown</u> to be making an appearance!"

Barbara has now gone through two utterances in Blamer Mode, both attacking Ruth Brown. Nora dislikes this and wants it to stop; she wants Barbara to know that she doesn't believe the statements about Ruth and is unwilling to gossip about her. So she says. . . .

NORA: "In a large company, it's impossible to know the basis for everyone else's work schedules. There's undoubtedly a logical explanation." (COMPUTING)

BARBARA: "<u>Sure</u> there is! The question is, what is she <u>doing</u> for the people in charge here that makes her an exception to the rules the rest of us have to follow? <u>That's</u> your expla<u>na</u>tion!"

NORA: "I see. You're saying that Ruth doesn't have to follow any of the company rules." (LEVELING)

110

BARBARA: "Well, no, I didn't say that!"

NORA: "I must have misunderstood you." (LEVELING)

BARBARA: "Yeah. You did."

NORA: "It's easy for misunderstandings to happen when people are busy and tired and wondering how they'll get through the day." (COMPUTING)

Nora has now cut this potential argument off without sacrificing any of her own principles, without catering to Barbara, and without letting herself be drawn into gossip. If Barbara has any social skills at all she'll understand that and will drop her attacks on Ruth Brown. But suppose she doesn't; suppose she is determined to continue. Then the scenario might go on like this, with Nora shifting between Computing and Leveling as each seems best to her:

BARBARA: "Hey, don't change the subject on me! I am sick and TIRED of the way Brown just comes and goes whenever she pleases! Aren't YOU?"

NORA: "I haven't noticed her doing that, Barbara."

BARBARA: "You're kidding! She does it all the TIME!"

NORA: "I hear you."

BARBARA: "Well? Don't you even CARE if she's getting away with murder?"

NORA: "No."

BARBARA: "You don't MEAN that!"

NORA: "Ruth has never inconvenienced me in any way, or caused me any problems; when I've needed her, she's always been available."

BARBARA: "But that's not the POINT!"

NORA: "Different people worry about different things, Barbara. Now how about giving me some of those copies? They're too heavy for you to carry all by yourself."

BARBARA: "Okay . . . thanks."

Certainly Barbara could once again refuse to drop the hostilities, especially if her metaphor is DISAGREEMENT IS COMBAT. She might carry on her attempt to provoke Nora into joining her in gossip—or into openly attacking her about it and serving as her opponent in a fight on the subject. If she does, Nora's strategy should be to continue using Leveler and Computer Modes as shown above, until Barbara wears out and gives up.

Every such episode tells Barbara clearly that Nora won't gossip with her. Every such episode *also* tells her that although Nora won't change the message she's sending she doesn't find it necessary to send it in a way that is humiliating or hurtful. If Barbara genuinely wants to discuss the problem of Ruth's schedule, she'll have to go to someone whose duties involve dealing with such issues. If, on the other hand, Barbara's real motive is to provoke Nora and "get her going" (see Chapter 8), it will become clear to her that that's not going to happen, and she'll drop it.

It's important to understand that Nora's intonation—the "way she's saying it"—is never sarcastic or vicious or patronizing. Suppose she said "DIFferent PEOPle worry about different THINGS, Barbara!"; that would be a different message. Say the line aloud, bearing down hard on the parts in capital letters—"DIF-" and "PEOP-" and "THINGS"—and listen carefully. The hostility is not in the words but in the tune, and Barbara will understand that that really means, "YOU worry about different THINGS than those $\underline{I}$ worry about, Barbara—and in my opinion the things YOU worry about are riDICulous!"

The time might come when Nora would be unwilling to make any further efforts to maintain a pleasant working relationship with Barbara. She might decide it wasn't worth any additional effort, and that she would settle for a disgruntled co-worker after all. In that case she can use Leveler Mode to state the plain truth, like this:

"Barbara, I have done everything I could think of to make it clear to you that I won't gossip about other people with you. I've done my best to tell you that in a respectful and courteous fashion. I'm through doing that now, because I've been unable to get through to you. Let's get things straight between us, therefore, so there won't be any more misunderstandings: Either you stop badmouthing people to me, or we have no further conversations. It's up to you."

112

Notice—this is a very negative message; its content is not likely to make Barbara happy. If it contained numerous extra emphatic stresses ("I have done EVerything I could THINK of to make it CLEAR to you . . .") it would be hostile language. But there's no hostility in it as written; it's a simple statement of Nora's feelings, perceptions, and intentions.

Nora has still another option open to her—that of finding something in Barbara's utterances that she can *agree* with. For example . . .

BARBARA: (leaning toward Nora and nudging her with one sharp elbow): "Well, look at <u>that</u>, will you? Unless my eyes are <u>fail</u>ing me, that is actually Ruth <u>Brown</u>, sitting at her <u>desk</u>!"

NORA: "What? I mean, why <u>wouldn't</u> she be at her desk?"

BARBARA: "<u>Well</u>, it's only twenty minutes after nine, <u>right</u>? That's very early <u>indeed</u> for Ms. <u>Brown</u> to be making an appearance!"

NORA: "Barbara, you're absolutely right—lateness is a real problem in the workplace. I must have read a dozen articles on that subject in business magazines this year, and nobody seems to have any useful ideas about how to handle it—whether it's best to ignore it, or to reward people for being on time, or punish them for being late . . . nothing seems to work on any reliable basis."

BARBARA: "Well . . . somebody ought to do something about <u>Ruth</u>, in my opinion."

NORA: "I'd be very interested in your ideas on the subject. What do you think should be done?"

Nora's strategy here is to continue to agree with Barbara on the abstract issue—that lateness is a problem in business—while refusing ever to respond to the specific issue of *Ruth Brown*'s behavior. This is an excellent way to go. Remember that one of the defining characteristics of hostile language is that it's intensely personal; shifting the focus of a discussion to an abstract issue will eliminate that characteristic.

The message Nora wants to get across to her colleague is, "I won't gossip with you about other people." She can just say so—

Leveling is one way to transmit the message, and it may become necessary. However, it will cause Barbara to lose face, and that's sure to introduce strain into the relationship between the two women. Suppose that instead Nora meets every attempt at gossip from Barbara by immediately shifting the focus from the personal to the abstract. That will convey the same message, with no sacrifice of Nora's principles or dignity, and without backing Barbara into any corners.

Which of these strategies Nora chooses will depend on many factors, including how patient she is, whether she likes or dislikes Barbara, how hard Barbara pushes to keep the disagreement going, and so on. What's most important is this:

> *Nora says what she does as a way of achieving goals that matter to her, and for what she perceives to be good strategic reasons—not by chance or by habit, and not just in unthinking reaction to something that Barbara says to her.*

Careful use of the Satir Modes is the best technique available for learning to communicate in that fashion.

7

USING PRESUPPOSITIONS

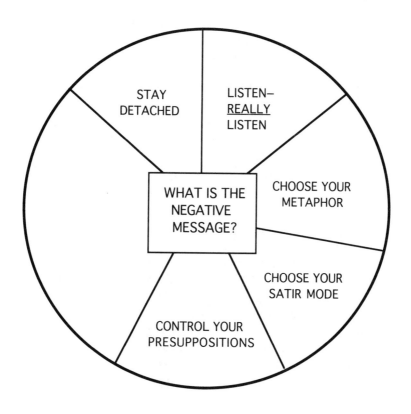

Scenario E

David looked at the man sitting across from him and sighed heavily; he looked down at the file folder on the desk and sighed again.

"Something wrong, Dave?" Tom asked.

"Yes," David said slowly. "Yes. Something's wrong." He hated this kind of thing, hated being stuck with the job of criticizing and complaining. *Why me?* he thought.

"Well?" Tom asked. "My sales figures are okay . . . they're better than okay, they're pretty darned <u>good</u>! So what's the problem?"

Get it over with, David told himself sternly. *Quit putting it off and just get it <u>done</u>!* He opened the folder, took a deep breath, and began.

"Tom," he said, "the problem is that you're <u>careless</u>. You keep making serious mistakes because you don't stop to check things out before you make a move. The rest of us keep having to clean up the messes you make. I'm sorry, but you have to clean up your <u>act</u>."

Tom leaned back in his chair and crossed his arms over his chest. His eyes narrowed, and he said, "Is <u>that</u> so? Well, give me an example! Just <u>one</u> mistake—give me just <u>one</u> <u>mess</u> somebody else had to clean up because of <u>me</u>!"

David was ready for that; he had a long list. Starting with the time Tom sent a contract to Apex Inc. with prices and terms that Apex didn't qualify for, prices and terms that had to be withdrawn. But he was careful; he didn't say one unnecessary word. Just "You did this, and then you did that, and what happened then was . . ." Just the facts.

He only got to item 6 before he was rudely interrupted.

"All right! All <u>right</u>!" Tom shouted, smacking the desk with his fist and shoving his chair back so that he could stand up and have a little yelling room. "You've made your <u>point</u>, buddy! I <u>get</u> it, all <u>right</u>? You can just stop right there—and you can get yourself another salesman for my <u>district</u>, too, because I'M not gonna BE here any longer!"

I knew this would happen, David thought sadly. *I warned them, but nobody would listen.*

116

"Now, Tom," he said, trying to sound casual, "<u>wait</u> a minute! Come on—sit down and let me finish, and then we can talk. All we want is for you to—"

"I don't give one thin DAMN what you want!" Tom bellowed. "I QUIT!" And he was out the door.

For the third time, David sighed. And then he picked up the phone and made the call he'd been sure he'd have to make. He understood why the boss felt that somebody had to tell Tom he was too careless, and that the rest of the sales force couldn't be expected to constantly deal with the consequences of his mistakes. But Tom was one of the best salesmen they had; they couldn't afford to lose him. Now somebody was going to have to try to convince him to stay on in spite of the criticism—*and* to be more careful—and that wasn't going to be easy. The only thing David was certain of was that the somebody was going to be somebody *else*, this time.

WHAT'S GOING ON HERE?

This situation is one in which we can feel sympathy for both parties involved; there are good things—and bad things—to be said on both sides of the issue.

Points of View

David has been dreading this encounter; he expected it to go badly and it did. So far as he's concerned, the argument was inevitable, in spite of the care he took to stay with the facts and add nothing else. He's just sorry that he had to be the designated driver for this particular communication collision.

*****

Tom's feelings about what happened have two parts. First, he's furious because he lost face. Tom knows what a good salesman he is, and he knows his value to the firm. The idea that one of the other sales reps could be instructed to chew him out about *any*thing makes him see red! Second, he feels a lot of guilt. He's not stupid; he knows his hasty actions have been creating problems for his colleagues. He's made a dozen resolutions to be more careful and is extremely touchy about his failure to keep them. The mixture of guilt and anger was more than he could handle, and now he knows he's made things much worse. He likes his job and doesn't want to quit, but he's drawn a line in the sand and you can't do that and then just back down like some kind of *wimp*!

****

This disagreeable interaction is of a type that most of us have to face from time to time. A teacher has to tell a student that his term paper isn't good enough. An employer has to tell a worker that her performance doesn't meet company standards. A club officer has to tell a member that he can't give the talk at the annual conference because his talks drive people away instead of bringing them in. A choir director has to tell a church member that her sour notes mean she can't be in the choir any longer. A mother has to tell a son that the pie he baked and is so proud of isn't edible. Most roles in life include negative messages like these, with a large potential for bringing on negative responses like Tom's in Scenario E.

In such situations, you need to use all the new information we've been discussing in previous chapters. And then you need to add a new technique. You need to put the power of *presuppositions* to work for you.

USING PRESUPPOSITIONS

Suppose you and I go to the first session of a course that we had hoped would be stimulating and challenging, and we are badly disappointed. Suppose I turn to you as we're leaving and say, "Even Chuck could pass this class!" We would both know that if that statement is true, two *other* statements also have to be true:

1. Chuck is a very poor student.

2. The class is ridiculously easy.

But notice that neither of those propositions is "there" in "Even Chuck could pass this class!" I didn't say "Even Chuck (whom everybody knows is a poor student) could pass this class (which everybody can see right away is ridiculously easy)." Those words weren't included in what I actually said. Nevertheless, like the "understood *you*" in "Eat your peas!" that your elementary school teacher talked about when you first studied commands, any fluent speaker of English knows they are part of its meaning. They aren't in the surface structure of the sentence, but English speakers all know they are in its deep structure. The technical name for such items—chunks of meaning that don't have to be given a surface shape in language because they can be taken for granted—is *presuppositions*.

The strategic use of presuppositions is a powerful technique that you can use whenever you need to build negative content into a message while at the same time decreasing its potential for hostility. We'll look at a number of ways to do this, and then at the end of the chapter we'll apply the technique to Scenario E.

TYPES OF PRESUPPOSITIONS

Now let's examine three types of presuppositions that I recommend for their effectiveness in reducing hostility, and one type that I strongly urge you to avoid. Examples of the first type are called *nominalizations*.

Nominalizations

The first grammar rule you ever learned was probably "Every sentence has to have a subject and a predicate." And you learned the rules that were supposed to explain how you knew what *kinds* of language sequences can take those roles. Nouns and other nominals can be subjects but not predicates; verbs and adjectives can be predicates but not subjects. However, although they probably were never explained to you, we have ways to get around these seeming restrictions. For example, we can *nominalize* verbs and adjectives, which means turning them into nounlike chunks that can qualify for subject status. We do this either by adding an "-ing" or by using special nominalized forms. For instance . . .

(Somebody) left . . .	Leaving can be difficult.
(Somebody is) lazy . . .	Laziness can be annoying.

You can't have a sentence with "left" or "lazy" as its subject; "Left can be difficult" or "Lazy can be annoying" aren't acceptable. But you can *nominalize* "left" or "lazy," use the results as subjects, and add predicates to them to make sentences like those shown above. This is an extremely valuable device for avoiding hostile language.

We've already seen one example of the usefulness of this pattern in "Another Look at Scenario D" on page 110. Barbara was determined to gossip about a colleague and was making a specific claim about her: "Ruth Brown is constantly late." Nora, to demonstrate that she wasn't willing to join in this, nominalized "late" and told Helen that they were in agreement about one thing: "Lateness is a problem in business." That let Nora move the discussion from a personal one specifically about Ruth Brown to an abstract one about "lateness."

Because one of the identifying characteristics of hostile language is the use of personal vocabulary, a switch to abstraction is always going to be helpful. A great deal of the time the result will also be a switch to Computer Mode, the most neutral of the Satir Modes. The basic principle is:

> Whenever you want to remove the personal element from a discussion, convert it to a more general issue by nominalizing its predicate.

Examples:

Personal issue:

"Your mother can't cook."

General response:

"It's amazing how important cooking has become in this country."

Personal issue:

"Why can't you ever put things where they belong?"

General response:

"Not being able to find things is really annoying."

Personal issue:

"Your Congressman is a hypocrite!"

General response:

"Hypocrisy has been a problem in Congress from the very beginning."

It's always possible that the person you're talking to will refuse to let the potential argument be defused so easily, especially if a verbal struggle would fill one of the personal needs such as the need for excitement or attention. But often a switch from the personal to the general is enough to transmit the message that you're unwilling to join the other person in an argument and at the same time change the subject smoothly. As in this dialogue:

ANN: "Mary, your mother can't cook. I can't <u>imagine</u> what she put <u>in</u> that soup we had for lunch!"

MARY: "It's amazing how important cooking has become in this country, isn't it?"

ANN: "Well, cooking <u>is</u> important!"

MARY: "I agree with you—it certainly is. And your husband tells me you're an expert on Chinese cooking."

ANN: "Oh, I wouldn't go <u>that</u> far!"

MARY: "I'll bet you could tell me why I can't make a decent egg drop soup. What I do is . . ."

Notice that in this dialogue the only negative message Mary has chosen is "I object to your behavior—I refuse to argue with you about my mother's cooking." If she also wanted to choose "and your facts are wrong," she could proceed like this . . .

121

ANN: "Mary, your mother can't cook. I can't <u>imagine</u> what she put <u>in</u> that soup we had for lunch!"

MARY: "Cooking is something very personal . . . Different people enjoy different kinds of food."

ANN: "I suppose that's true. Maybe your family <u>likes</u> that soup."

MARY: "We do; it's one of our favorites. And your husband tells me that you're an expert on Chinese cooking . . ." (And so on)

Making a nominalization more detailed will give it additional strength. English presupposes that anything "owned" exists; as a result, adding a possessive gives your presupposition more weight. If I want you to know that I have a new car, I can tell you so by claiming that it's true, straight out; I can just say, "I have a new car." But I can also use nominalization to *presuppose* that it's true, like this:

"My new car is fun to drive." Or . . .

"My new green car with the mag wheels is fun to drive."

The more elaborate the description gets, the more strongly the sentence presupposes that I really do have a new car. As in, "My new green car with the mag wheels, the one I bought from that dealer in New Bedford while I was on vacation, is fun to drive." I've stopped claiming that I have a new car, I'm taking that for granted, and I'm claiming only that it's fun to drive.

How does this help you with negative messages? *Anything you don't want to argue about should be sheltered inside a presupposition if possible; the stronger the presupposition is, the less likely an argument becomes.* Compare these examples:

- "You're frequently late, and that worries people."
- "Your frequent lateness worries people."

Similar as these two sentences are, they do different things. The first one makes two open claims: that the person spoken to is frequently late and that this worries people. The second sentence *presupposes* that the person is frequently late; it claims only that this flaw—which in this format everyone knows can just be taken for granted—worries people. You can check this out by noticing how the statements would be contradicted:

- "You are constantly late, and that worries people."

  Contradiction: "I am <u>not</u> constantly late!"

- "Your constant lateness worries people."

  Contradiction: "It does <u>not</u> worry people!"

To give presuppositional shelter to a statement that would otherwise be an open negative claim, follow these three steps:

Step One: Nominalize its predicate.

Step Two: Make the nominalization as elaborate as is appropriate, using possessive and descriptive details.

Step Three: Add a new predicate—the vaguer and more innocuous the better—to finish your sentence.

It's not that those who hear you say "Your constant lateness worries people" don't *know* that "You are constantly late" is part of its meaning. Of course they know. But this structure, *by not making a direct and open negative claim about the person spoken to*, decreases the loss of face for that person. It has as part of its metamessage something like this: "I have to make a negative comment about you, but notice that I'm doing it in a respectful manner." With rational people, that helps, especially when—as is usually true—they realize that you're only criticizing them because you can't avoid doing so.

You don't have to worry about the technical details of nominalization, by the way. Long before teachers made you memorize the rules about what can be subjects and what can be predicates, you were demonstrating that you *knew* those rules. Every time you said a sentence, you proved that. Similarly, although you can't recite the rules for nominalizing, you know them perfectly. You would instantly reject "Your frequent latement" or "His constant lazyation" as non-English. You can trust your internal grammar for matters of this kind, always.

Presuppositions of Time

Another kind of presupposition you can use to reduce hostility in a negative message is found in many English words and phrases that specify *time*. Suppose you find yourself facing an interaction with one of your employees—let's call him Joe—that you're pretty sure will go like this:

JOE: "I don't <u>want</u> to go to Bleeperton. I <u>hate</u> the place."

YOU: "I know. But you <u>have</u> to go to Bleeperton, no matter <u>how</u> you feel about it."

If Joe's going to go on working for you, you have to make it clear to him that he can't pick and choose his assignments; those choices are up to *you*. But you can use time words to carry that negative message in a more positive way. For example . . .

JOE: "I don't <u>want</u> to go to Bleeperton. I <u>hate</u> the place."

YOU: "I know. After you get back, you'll be glad it's over."

—or—

YOU: "I know. When you're there, you'll be thinking how much nicer it is here in Florida in the winter."

—or—

YOU: "I know you do. While you're there, would you rather stay at the Holiday Inn or someplace closer to the airport?"

These time words—"after, when, while"—presuppose that X *will* go to Bleeperton, making it possible for you to avoid stating the open claim: "You <u>have</u> to go, no matter how you feel about it."

That claim carries a metamessage with it saying, *"I'm the boss and I have the right to give you orders and there's nothing you can do about it."* That's a Leveling statement; it's true, and you have every right to say it. But it means a major loss of face for your employee. In the time word examples the message is still *there*, and the

124

employee is fully aware of it. But the metamessage of dominance is far less harsh and obvious, and it has an added piece that says, "Notice that I am giving you this message in a respectful manner." The resulting loss of face for Joe is much diminished.

This is *not* being a wimp—let's emphasize that and settle it. The only reason for deliberately causing someone to lose face in a disagreement is to establish two points: You are the winner, and that person is the loser. You may find yourself forced to do that sometimes, but it's poor strategy to *start* an interaction that way unless you have excellent reasons for humiliating the person you're speaking to. Most people construct negative messages as direct negative claims from habit and an unconscious acceptance of the DISAGREEMENT IS COMBAT metaphor; you don't have to follow their lead. First try more positive structures; if they fail you, you can always move on to Leveling and direct confrontation when that becomes clear.

"As You Know . . ." Presuppositions

A dermatologist once asked me for help because he kept finding himself in disagreements with doctors from other specialties. They would call him up, tell him, "I've got a patient here with psoriasis," and ask him what they should prescribe. The dermatologist didn't want to offend his colleagues; on the other hand, he didn't agree with them that nondermatologists can be trusted to identify psoriasis accurately. "They think psoriasis is so obvious that anybody at all can identify it easily," he told me, "and that's just not true. But when I say so, they get mad. What should I say to them?"

English has a set of predicates—including "know" and "be aware"—that are called *factives* because the statements that follow them in a sentence are presupposed to be "true facts." I explained to the doctor that factives would help him avoid the disagreements and suggested that he use sequences like these:

"As you know, many other skin disorders look almost exactly like psoriasis."

"As you are aware, even dermatologists sometimes have a hard time diagnosing psoriasis, because it looks so much like many other skin disorders."

"As I know you are aware, psoriasis is a tricky diagnosis—and prescribing for it when the condition is really something else could lead to serious problems."

The doctor called me back a few weeks later to tell me that this strategy had solved his problem.

There are times when you need to tell someone something they ought to know already, but they either don't know it, have forgotten it, or are pretending not to know it. In such situations, all of the following are hostile language and are likely to provoke an argument:

- "I can't believe that you don't know ..."

- "Don't tell me you don't KNOW ..."

- "For crying out loud! You don't even know ..."

- "Hmmm. You've obviously forgotten that ..."

- "I hate to have to say this, but you must have forgotten that ..."

Don't say any of those things. Just say, "As you know ..." or "As you are aware ..." or "As all of us in this meeting realize ..." and follow it up with the necessary piece of information. If your listener really doesn't know or has forgotten, the information gap will then have been filled, with no loss of face. If your listener *does* know, you've simply acknowledged that fact and no harm is done.

PRESUPPOSITIONS TO AVOID

Not all presuppositions are suitable strategies for avoiding negative effects, of course. There are some that I call Trojan Horses because, however innocent they seem on the surface, they're packed with hostile potential. Even when you're convinced that you mean them innocently, it's best to avoid them, because the chances are so strong that anyone hearing you use them will leap to the conclusion that your intentions are hostile.

Not long ago I read in a magazine for law enforcement professionals that a percentage of all women interviewed by the police in a given period "admitted having been beaten" by their male partners. That's not a neutral comment, and it's a symptom of the attitude many police departments have toward domestic violence; people only "admit" things about which they feel guilty and/or ashamed. The verb "admit" presupposes that guilt and shame. "You'd admit that you've been late a lot, wouldn't you?" is hostile language that cannot be made less so by a subsequent "Hey, all I <u>said</u> was . . ." It's a Trojan Horse, and it should be avoided.

Here are some more Trojan horses, with examples:

- "I'm so glad that you managed to get your grant."

Manage to X presupposes that the individual had a great deal of difficulty getting X done; it's not complimentary.

- "Everyone on the committee was more than willing to humor you about that part of the agreement."

To *humor* someone is to behave toward them as you would behave toward a child or a person not in full possession of their senses. "Indulge" and "cater to" are just as bad. If you can't avoid a message like this, say that everyone was willing to "defer to your wishes," which moves the focus from the individual personally to his or her "wishes."

- "It's wonderful that you've finally been promoted!"

The problem here is with *finally*, which—in a context like this— does the same sort of damage that "I'm so glad you managed to get promoted" would do. Worst of all is the combined hostility of "It's wonderful that you've finally managed to" do whatever has been accomplished; the only possible reason for saying that is to be deliberately hostile.

Finally, be very careful with the use of nominalizations that turn predicates not into subjects but into what teachers insist on calling "predicate nominatives." For example:

Original claim:

"You tell lies."

(Subject, "you"; predicate, "tell lies.")

127

Revision with nominalization of the predicate:

"You are a liar."

(Subject, predicate (with a "predicate nominative"),

"are a liar.")

In "You're a failure," "a failure" is the predicate nominative, created by nominalizing "You fail." And the strong implication of sentences like "You're a liar" and "You're a failure" is that the person *always* does whatever was nominalized. Whether that is precisely what you intended to say isn't relevant; the implication is there in the language.

The child who has told you one lie needs to be informed that that's not acceptable and won't be tolerated—but one lie doesn't make the child a liar. The adult who has failed in business may need to know that you have a negative reaction to that fact—but one failed business doesn't make the person "a failure."

Certainly there are times when "manage" and "humor" and all the rest can be used appropriately and without conveying hostility; it depends on the specific circumstances at the time they're used. You can depend on your mental grammar to let you know when they're safe and when they're not. But you have to stay aware of their *potential* for hostility, so that you'll think about them before you use them. When in doubt, use something else in their place.

When you have had some lead time—as David did in Scenario E—and you know you're going to have to deliver a critical message, sit down and write out what you plan to say. Look it over carefully; say it aloud and listen to it. Ask yourself: *What does that mean—exactly?*" Make certain that you haven't unintentionally dropped in some word or phrase that carries hostile presuppositions with it.

SHE SAYS/HE SAYS

Both men and women use presuppositions as strategic moves in communication, in both positive and negative ways. No evidence exists that either gender is more skilled at this, or more inclined to abuse the technique. There will be differences, but they are *individual* differences, not gender differences. This doesn't mean that gender can be dismissed as irrelevant in this context, however.

Despite all the lip service given to the idea of gender equality, we still tend to react stereotypically when language is used to attack across gender lines, especially when the attack is made publicly. A man's attack on a woman still makes us uneasy because it seems unchivalrous and like "dirty pool." To avoid that reaction, the skilled attacker is careful to hide his negative messages inside presuppositions instead of making them openly. Let's look at a real world example of this phenomenon.

In January 1996 William Safire wrote a column about Hillary Clinton that appeared in newspapers all over the country. His opening sentence became a point of nationwide discussion. It was:

> "Americans of all political persuasions are coming to the sad realization that our first lady—a woman of undoubted talents who was a role model for many in her generation—is a congenital liar."

Safire's necessary negative message, one that he could view as appropriate to his role as a journalist who pulls no punches and does no special favors, was "I believe that Americans of all political persuasions now know that Hillary Clinton has told a number of lies." Whether that's true or not is not the issue here; he had every right to say that it was what he *believed*. However, that's *not* what he said. He added three extra chunks of meaning, using nominalizations.

First, he turned "Americans have come to realize that Hillary has told a number of lies" into "Americans are coming to the realization that . . ." with "the realization is sad" thrown in to make it more venomous. (The image is of good and moral American men and women sitting around wiping away tears as the knowledge of Hillary Clinton's wickedness overwhelms them.) Second, "Hillary Clinton has told lies" became "Hillary Clinton is a liar." And then, to finish it off, Safire added that her status as a liar was "congenital." That let him presuppose "Hillary Clinton was a liar from the moment she was born, and the condition was inherited," something he presumably would not have dared to say as an open claim. Using presuppositions let him insult not only the First Lady but her family as well, for as far back as he cared to stretch it.

None of these extra messages was necessary. He could have accomplished his objective as guardian of the public morals by sticking to "I am convinced that Hillary Clinton has told a number of lies." The purpose of the rest of it was to express as forcefully as possible his deep objections to Hillary Clinton personally, as contemptuously and disrespectfully as possible. He succeeded in doing that—and in getting away with it, in spite of the widespread American feeling that badmouthing a woman publicly is unacceptable.

Safire isn't a gracious winner; he wasn't quite through with Mrs. Clinton. In his next column he reported that "Dukes-up faxes and calls reveal a gender difference in reader reaction: 90 percent who say 'you are an obnoxious boor' are women, and 90 percent who say 'it's about time somebody said what she was' are men." And he went on to bemoan the dilemma that journalists and citizens face when they need to say that a woman has told lies. AS IF he were too ignorant of his native language to know that the problem is not in "has told lies" but in "is a congenital liar."

Notice also that his description of comments from male readers is not that they said "It's about time somebody said what she has done," which would be negative but not hostile and would be comments about Hillary's actions. Instead, he reports them as having told him that "It's about time somebody said what she was."

I suggest that—to examine the use of presuppositions employed for no other purpose than to be as hostile as possible—you read both of Safire's columns and analyze them carefully. The columns appeared in the *New York Times* (and many other newspapers) on January 9th and 11th of 1996.

ANOTHER LOOK AT SCENARIO E

DAVID: "Tom, the problem is that you're <u>careless</u>. You keep making serious mistakes because you don't stop to check things out before you make a move. The rest of us keep having to clean up the messes you make. I'm sorry, but you have to clean up your <u>act</u>."

This is how David begins his interaction with Tom, after having agreed with him that "something is wrong." David's utterance is basically Leveling, and is composed of three direct accusations and a direct command. And when Tom——already on the defensive—demands examples, David proceeds to read him a list of them.

It could have been worse. David could have done this in Blamer Mode, starting out with "Tom, everybody here has HAD it with you! You're so CAREless you're like a loose cannon—you can't be BOThered to stop and think before you make your moves, you just do whatever the blazes comes into your head and leave it to everybody ELSE to clean up the MESSes you make! You're way out of LINE, Tom, and . . ." And so on. He didn't do that. But his own linguistic instincts had told him, in advance, that what he *did* do, moderate and rational as it was, would end with Tom storming out of the session in a rage. He should have heeded the warnings of his mental grammar and handled this encounter differently.

Let's take each of the troublesome chunks and rewrite it so that it would be less like waving a red cape at a bull. We'll do it in several stages, to make the revision process more clear.

First Stage

1. "The problem is that you're <u>careless</u>."

1a. "Your carelessness is a problem."

2. "You keep making mistakes because you don't stop to check things out before you make a move."

2a. "Not checking things out before making a move causes your mistakes."

3. "The rest of us keep having to clean up the messes you make."

3a. "Cleaning up the messes you make is something the rest of us keep having to do."

4. "Clean up your <u>act</u>."

4a. "When you've cleaned up your act, things will improve."

4b. "When you've had a chance to correct all this, things will go more smoothly."

Second Stage

1a. "Your carelessness is a problem."

131

1b. "Carelessness can be a problem."

2a. "Not checking things out before making a move causes your mistakes."

2b. "Not checking things out before making a move is a mistake."

3a. "Cleaning up the messes you make is something the rest of us keep having to do."

3b. "Cleaning up somebody else's messes can be a burden."

4a. "When you've cleaned up your act, things will improve."

4b. "When you've had a chance to correct all this, things will go more smoothly."

In this second stage, we've gotten rid of a lot of the personal vocabulary—"you, your, us," etc. This decreases the level of potential hostility. Tom knows David is talking to him and about his performance—the "you's" aren't necessary. Because "clean up your act" carries a lot of semantic contamination, we've replaced it with the more neutral "correct all this."

Third Stage

1c/2c. "Carelessness, and not checking things out before making a move, can cause problems."

3c. "And dealing with the consequences of those problems can be a burden."

4c. "Things will go more smoothly after you've had a chance to make some changes."

And let's do one more thing—let's get rid of the opening sequence in which David answers Tom's "Is something wrong?" with "Yes. Yes. Something's wrong." Everything about David's opening, including his body language, was setting the session up for the failure he was sure was coming; we can fix that. Like this:

TOM: "Something wrong, Dave?"

DAVID: "Nothing serious, Tom, and nothing you can't easily take care of."

TOM: "Okay. What's up?"

DAVID: "Tom, as you and I both know, carelessness, and not checking things out before making a move, can cause problems. And dealing with the consequences of those problems can be a burden."

TOM: "Right. (Pause.) Like when I give a customer prices off the top of my head and they turn out to be the wrong figures. Is that what you're getting at?"

DAVID: "That kind of thing . . . sure."

TOM: "They told you to talk to me about it, huh?"

DAVID: "That's right. I haven't been looking forward to it."

TOM: "Look, I get wound up in making a deal and I lose track of the details; I know that. And I know it's been a pain for other people around here. I'd already realized that I have to make some changes. No problem."

DAVID: "I knew it wouldn't be."

And suppose Tom doesn't help David out that much—suppose he doesn't volunteer an example of his carelessness so easily?

DAVID: "Tom, as you and I both know, carelessness, and not checking things out before making a move, can cause problems. And dealing with the consequences of those problems can be a burden."

TOM: "Right. So?"

DAVID: "Well, for example, prices have to be checked before a customer hears about them—otherwise, things get mixed up. People get upset. Problems come along. Right?"

TOM: "Like that time I got the figures wrong with Ammex."

DAVID: "That kind of thing . . . sure."

The negative message that David has to get across to Tom is just "You're careless when you make deals, and we want you to change that." He can do that just as easily by focusing on the prices as by focusing on Tom. Saying "Prices have to be checked before a customer hears about them" will serve just as well to transmit the necessary message as "You have to check the prices before you quote them to a customer." "Carelessness is a problem" is just as effective as "The problem is that you're careless." But these simple changes let Tom save face and keep him from feeling that he is obligated to *fight*. Even if it takes a little more time for David to plan what he'll say, and a little more time in the session itself, this strategy *saves* time in the long run—because nobody has to deal with a top salesman who is furious and humiliated and yelling "I QUIT!" If this approach doesn't work, there will be plenty of opportunities later to deliver the message more harshly.

8

MANAGING THE ENGLISH VERBAL ATTACK PATTERNS

Scenario F

Cheryl had expected her mother- and father-in-law to be surprised; she'd been braced for them to be a little upset about the move to Fairview. But she'd never dreamed they would react the way they <u>did</u>! The fight started with a horrified "But <u>who's</u> going to look after <u>Sam</u>?"—as if she and Sam would ever accept one of those "long-distance marriage" arrangements!—and it went downhill from there.

"<u>Wait</u> a minute," she said tensely, as soon as she was able to get a word in. "I don't think you understand! My new job will start at $65,000 a year—that's ten thousand more than I make now."

"It's a terrific opportunity, Dad," Sam put in from his end of the table.

But Carl ignored him and concentrated on Cheryl. "Oh, <u>we</u> understand!" he shouted at her. "We may not have fancy <u>law</u> degrees like <u>you</u> and <u>Sam</u> have, but we're not IGnorant! We understand PERfectly! We understand that you are a selfish woman who cares nothing about anybody but herSELF, Cheryl! We understood THAT the minute you told us you wouldn't be giving us any GRANDchildren! And if you think Louise and I are just going to lie down and let you RUIN our son's CAREER, you'd better think AGAIN!"

"Oh, come on, <u>Dad</u>!" Sam protested. "You and Mom could at least TRY to act like rational adults! I can get another position in two days flat—YOU know THAT!"

Louise turned and glared at her son. "That's not the POINT!" she snapped, and she turned back to Cheryl before he could say another word. "Cheryl," she said, white-faced and tightlipped, "if you really LOVED Sam, YOU wouldn't even CONSIDER taking a job in another city! Even a woman like YOU knows better than THAT!"

"And if YOU had the brains you were BORN with," Carl flung at Sam, "you'd put your FOOT down and tell your wife to count her blessings right here where she IS!"

It was too much for Cheryl; she had reached the end of her patience. She knew people still existed who thought that men should move to better jobs even if it meant a job change for their wives, but who wouldn't accept it the other way around. She and

136

Sam would have been willing to sit down and discuss that issue and explain that they didn't see things that way. But Carl and Louise had gone too far now, and the opportunity for discussion had been thrown away. She wasn't *about* to let them get away with the vicious things they were saying!

"Just exactly what do you <u>mean</u>—a woman like me?" she demanded. "What do you MEAN—IF I loved Sam?! How DARE you say such things, to EITHER ONE of us! I have sat here and listened to you both, and I have tried to stay courteous in spite of your abuse, but there are LIMits! And now <u>I</u> have a few things to say to YOU!"

WHAT'S GOING ON HERE?

This kind of no-holds-barred disagreement is like a fire in a wooden barn filled with dry hay: It feeds on itself and it burns right down to the bare ground.

POINTS OF VIEW

Cheryl is an excellent lawyer; she intends to go straight to the top of the legal profession and she works hard at it. When the new job offer came her way, she and Sam sat down and discussed it carefully and decided—together—that she should accept. Cheryl is proud of the new opportunity and very happy about it; she knew that Sam's parents would be sorry to see them move away, but she assumed that when they understood what a move upward the change would be they'd accept it and be happy too. She is horrified now, deeply hurt, and prepared to put her considerable courtroom skills to work immediately to demonstrate to Carl and Louise that she can outdo them in verbal violence any day of the week and twice on Sundays.

*****

The way Sam sees things, Cheryl's job change is wonderful news. He's right about how easy it will be for him to find another position; like Cheryl, his skills as a lawyer mean that he can write his own ticket.

He can hardly wait to move on. He was a little more uneasy about his parents' reaction to their moving *away* than Cheryl was, because he knows how high a value they put on such things as regular Sunday dinners with their kids. He was even prepared for a certain amount of fireworks, because he's seen Carl and Louise in this kind of fight before. But it was worse than he had thought it would be, by far, and he's very sorry that the situation got so badly out of control. It spoils the pleasure he and Cheryl have felt about the move, and it's going to be hard to mend fences now between his wife and his parents.

*****

Carl and Louise perceive the situation very differently. They've been willing to accept the fact that Cheryl wants to continue working for now, but their hope has been that this would wear off—after all, Sam can earn more than enough money to support the family—and that she'd then stay home and provide them with a grandchild or two. They are appalled at the idea that she would actually take a job in another city, meaning that Sam would have to leave *his* law firm and tag along after her. This strikes them as the most unnatural and warped kind of behavior. The husband's career *must* come first—they both believe that with all their hearts. In their shock they are attacking Cheryl viciously as a way of defending their son, without giving any thought to what such an attack might mean for their relationship with Cheryl and Sam in the future. They are both victims of the "emotional hijacking" phenomenon discussed on page 44, and have reacted to Cheryl as if she were a saber-toothed tiger rather than a daughter-in-law.

THE ENGLISH VERBAL ATTACK PATTERNS

When we find ourselves in fights like this one we don't have to worry about how we'll think up terrible things to say. We have a whole set of hostile language patterns on automatic pilot that make it easy for us to make spectacles of ourselves. These are the *Verbal Attack Patterns of English*—VAPs for short. In Scenario F the attackers are relying on those patterns, along with unbroken Blaming Mode. Here are the VAP examples from the scenario:

SAM: "You and Mom could at least TRY to act like rational adults!"

LOUISE: "If you really LOVED Sam, YOU wouldn't even CONSIDER taking a job in another city!"

LOUISE: "Even a woman like YOU knows better than THAT!"

CARL: "If YOU had the brains you were BORN with, you'd put your FOOT down and tell your wife to count her blessings right here where she IS!"

Like the grammar rules that you use to generate English questions and commands and promises and threats (and all your other utterances), you *know* the rules for generating the set of verbal attacks—but you're not consciously aware of them and you can't recite or explain them. Matters are made worse by the fact that most people react negatively to the very phrase "grammar rule." I understand this reaction, which is a product of the irrational way our schools teach grammar, but I regret the emotional barrier it poses to understanding language and communication.

As you read the discussion below, remember that your long-term memory includes a *flawless* grammar of your native language, and that this fact is totally independent of the grades you got when you were obliged to study English grammar. You wouldn't expect to get a driver's license by reciting the rules for building a car; it's equally absurd to expect people to demonstrate that they know a language by reciting its rules. You prove that you know how to drive a car by driving it; you prove that you know how to use a language by using it—by speaking, writing, reading, and understanding it. We have to discuss the English VAPs in order to tackle the myths and distortions that have built up around them over time. But I promise you that your flawless internal grammar will carry most of the weight.

RECOGNIZING THE VERBAL ATTACK PATTERNS

When I gave the examples of VAPs from the scenario, I'm sure you recognized them instantly. You know those patterns. You hear them used everywhere you go, and you undoubtedly use them yourself at least once in a while. The fact that you "know them when you hear them" (or read them) tells you that you know the rules with which they are constructed. Here are the basics.

♦ VAPs have two parts: an obvious and open hostile sequence whose purpose is to get the listener's attention, called the *bait*; and one or more less obvious hostile sequences that are sheltered in presuppositions. In some of these the division between the two parts is very clear; in others they are mingled in complicated ways.

Example: Suppose the VAP is, "If you REALLY cared about your health, YOU wouldn't SMOKE three packs of cigarettes a day!" The bait is "You smoke three packs of cigarettes a day," and "If you REALLY cared about your health" shelters the less obvious presupposed insult, "You don't really care about your health."

♦ VAPs are learned early in childhood just like any other part of the language; the less subtle ones are used with skill by tiny kids.

Example: "If you REALLY love me, YOU won't MAKE me eat your nasty broccoli!" If this appears as "If oo WEALLY wuv me, won't MAKE me eat nasty bwoccowi!", the fact that the child can't give it an adult pronunciation doesn't make it any less an attack.

♦ VAPs usually have an identical counterpart—that is, a sequence with exactly the same *words*—that is not an attack. The difference between the two is not in the words but in the tune the words are set to.

Example: "Some fathers would be upset if their kids forgot to send a Father's Day card" is a neutral statement of the speaker's opinion. However, "SOME fathers would be upSET if their kids forgot to send a FATHER'S Day card!" is an attack.

♦ People who use VAPs aren't ordinarily interested in the response they would get if they used the otherwise identical nonattack sequence. For example, if the VAP has the form of a question, the attacker isn't usually interested in its answer. Chronic VAPpers use VAPs to get and keep their targeted victim's attention and to provoke emotional reactions that serve as evidence that that has happened. This is their total purpose; everything else is just "an unfortunate and unavoidable side effect."

140

Example: (a) "Why do you eat so much junk food?" is not an attack but a request for information from someone who wants to know the answer. It may be a *rude* question, but it's only a question, nothing more. (b) "WHY do you eat SO MUCH JUNK food?" This is an attack, and is set to a different tune. The attacker couldn't care less why the potential victim eats junk food.

✦ VAPs are based on scripts that we learn as children and that are automatic by the time we reach our teens; they are action chains. Like all action chains, if they are interrupted they are *over* unless the people involved are willing to start them again from the beginning.

Example: If you respond to "YOU'RE not the ONly person that hates to do DISHES, you know!" with "You're absolutely right," the VAP attack is over. That's your best response, since the chances that you *are* the only person who hates to do dishes are close to zero—but it's not the next line in the script. The attacker is waiting for you to say something like "Listen, I do TWICE as many dishes as YOU do!"

✦ Not all examples of hostile language are VAPs, but all VAPs are examples of hostile language.

Example: "You're a CREEP!" is hostile language and so is "I can't STAND people that use handicapped parking spaces when there's nothing WRONG with them at ALL!"—but neither of those utterances is from the set of VAPs. They don't have the other identifying characteristics of the patterns.

The two simplest and earliest learned VAPs are the "If you/If you really" pattern and the one that begins with a heavily emphasized "WHY." For example:

• "If you REALLY cared about your kids, YOU wouldn't PUT them in DAYcare!"

• "If you really LOVED your kids, YOU wouldn't THINK of smoking when they're around!"

141

- "If you CARED about your job, YOU'D get to work on TIME once in a while!"
- "If you had any REAL concern for what happens in this country, YOU'D quit griping and GET out and VOTE!"
- "WHY can't you follow even the SIMPlest inSTRUCTIONS?"
- "WHY don't you ever think about ANYbody but yourSELF?"
- "WHY are you ALways LATE?"

As is obvious from these examples—and the many others that you could produce if you were asked to do so—it's their melodies that we recognize, not their words. We demonstrate our skill with the grammar of English verbal violence by knowing exactly how to plug in the words and give them emphatic stresses so that the tunes will be the ones we recognize as VAPs.

I can't tell you exactly how many VAPs English has; I can't give you a list and assure you that it's complete. I've been working with the VAPs since the late 1960s (starting with a set of eight very common ones that I found almost immediately), and every once in a while I find another one, or one is pointed out to me. My estimate is that there are no more than twenty-five in the set, and probably fewer than that. But it doesn't matter, because the *complete* set is in your internal grammar, and you know them when you hear them. What does matter is that you become aware that they exist and that there is a simple technique for dealing with them.

RESPONDING TO THE VERBAL ATTACK PATTERNS

Linguistically the procedure for responding to VAPs could hardly be simpler. You have just two rules:

Rule One:

Ignore the bait, no matter how outrageous.

Rule Two:

Respond to one of the other presupposed parts of the sequence instead.

The problem people have with this is not in constructing the messages, but in resisting the temptation to wade right into the fray and *fight*. They say to me, "But what he (*or she*) said to me was so mean!" And I ask them, "When you go fishing, do you take boring bait?" Of *course* the bait will be mean; that's to be expected. Because verbal attackers have learned that the meaner the bait is, the more likely it is that the intended victim will take it and run with it.

Suppose you are someone with a chronic disability that isn't obvious to others but makes it impossible for you to walk more than very short distances. You pull into a handicapped parking space at the mall on a day when the parking lot is absolutely packed. And as you step out of your car, another shopper hits the brakes right in front of you and he challenges you with this VAP:

"YOU'RE not the ONly person that needs a PARKing space, you know!"

This pattern is one of the complicated ones; little children don't use it much, and when they try they usually get it wrong, because it relies heavily on context and its parts aren't easy to separate. The bait is the accusation that you're behaving as if you were the only person in the world who needed a parking space, to such an extent that you're taking a handicapped space you're not entitled to use. The sheltered insult is that you're fully aware of your disgusting behavior, you creep.

In our society, your natural inclination is going to be to counterattack, which will lead to something like this:

MAN: "YOU'RE not the ONly person that needs a PARKing space, you know!"

YOU: "LISTen, I have a SERious HEALTH problem!"

MAN: "Oh, SURE you do! And pigs FLY!"

YOU: "Are YOU calling ME a LIAR?"

MAN: "If the shoe FITS, lady, WEAR IT!"

(And so on.)

However this ends—even if it doesn't end with the mall's security guards being called to break it up—both you and the attacker will have wasted a lot of time in an ugly public fight. The difference between the two of you is that the VAPper—but not you—will have *enjoyed* the episode. You will have gained nothing at all, and the stress of the argument will have taken its toll on you. The VAPper, however, will have gained exactly what he was after when he decided to pick the fight.

One of the presuppositions of "YOU'RE not the ONly person that needs a PARKing space, you know!" is the empty logical one—"There are other people besides you who need a parking space." And that is what you should respond to. Refuse to agree that you're a disgusting creep who steals handicapped parking spaces, and refuse to play the VAPper's foolish game, by saying, "You're absolutely right" and going on with your own plans without further ado.

At this point I know from long experience that you're almost certainly thinking my recommendation is all wrong because it "lets him get AWAY with it!" That's an understandable reaction, but it's an error.

Consider the situation. You had a plan and a goal: to go to the shopping mall and buy whatever it was you were shopping for. The man who challenged you had a plan and a goal, too: to get and keep your attention and provoke an emotional reaction from you that would be evidence of his power to carry out his agenda. *Without your attention and your emotional reaction, he can't get what he wants.* When you join in the VAP session and play the role of victim for him, THAT—not ignoring his outrageous remarks—is letting him get away with it. If you understand that, you'll be able to get his opening challenge past your amygdala sentry to the thinking part of your brain and you won't get caught in an absurd emotional hijacking.

People who use VAPs aren't always primitive hackers and slashers. Sometimes they're quite subtle; sometimes they put "dear" at the beginning of the attack and "sweetheart" at the end, to distract the listener. And sometimes they're just not very bright, and the rule about picking on people your own size has to be observed. In many such cases you can use a device called "The Boring Baroque Response." Suppose you have adopted a child of a different ethnic background, and you're sitting in an airport with that child. A woman comes up to you and says, "If you REALLY cared about that child, YOU'D want him to grow up with his own KIND!"

Certainly you will be tempted to follow the script and take the lady on. Lines about minding her own business, and who the expletive does she think she is talking to you like that, and what you think of bigots, will come easily to your mind. But if you say those things we know what the outcome will be: You'll be upset when it's over; your child will have had a lengthy lesson in the use of hostile language; and the woman will have gotten exactly what she wanted from you. Don't do it. Instead, use the Boring Baroque Response, directed at the empty presupposition that this person wants to hear you answer her. Like this:

> "You know, hearing you say that reminds me of something I read only the other day in the *New York Times*. No, wait a minute—it couldn't have been the *Times*, because I haven't gotten around to reading it this week, it must have been the *Washington Post*. Or it could have been the *Wall Street Journal*, come to think of it, because . . ."

(And so on.)

The Boring Baroque Response (BBR) is based on a number of experiences I had on Greyhound buses when I was young; I'm sure you've had similar encounters with people who can't give you directions to the corner without telling you every move they've made since they got up that morning, in excruciating detail. Very early in the BBR your attacker will back off, say "Oh, NEVer MIND!," and go away. You can then turn to your child, say, "See, honey? That's one way to handle situations like that," and catch your plane.

It's absolutely critical to remember that any response to a VAP has to be made neutrally—set to a neutral tune. When a response is sarcastic or patronizing or insolent, it's hostile language, no matter what words it contains.

Here are three more of the common VAPs, with suggested responses.

• "EVen a person YOUR age ought to know SOMEthing about rock music!"

Don't say: "Whadda you MEAN, a person 'my age'?" THERE'S nothing WRONG with my age, young man! And I know more about rock music than you can ever HOPE to know!" Say "The idea that people my age are somehow limited is an idea you run into once in a while." If you like the youngster, you can add, "I'm surprised to hear it from you" or "I'm sorry you feel that way."

- "If you REALLY wanted to get ahead in this firm, YOU wouldn't WANT to take every weekend off while the rest of us work!"

Don't say, "Just because YOU'RE a workaholic, buddy, that doesn't mean EVERYbody has to be! If YOU'RE such a sucker that they can con you into working weekends, that's YOUR business— I'M not that STUPid!" Go to Computer Mode and say "The idea that people can control their desires by willpower alone has a certain appeal." Or go to Leveler Mode and say, "Sure I want to get ahead here; it matters a lot to me."

- "Don't you EVen CARE if little children are STARVING all over the WORLD?"

This is one of the most complex of the VAPs; the bait here, triggered by the mysterious word "even," isn't the part about the starving children. It's simply, "You're despicable; you're beneath contempt." Don't say, "Listen, I care JUST AS much about starving children as YOU do! What makes you think YOU'RE Mother Theresa?" Say, "Every thinking person today is concerned about world hunger."

In every case, the strategy is the same: Ignore the bait and respond, neutrally, to some other part of the utterance. Like depriving a fire of oxygen, this deprives the VAPper of the fuel he or she has to have to go on with the argument.

SHE SAYS/HE SAYS

There is no evidence that either gender is more likely to use the verbal attack patterns than the other; they're part of the basic grammar of English and are used by everyone. There *is* evidence that most men tend to have a more intense physiological reaction to VAP sessions than most women do. This may be because men, in the context of the perceived cultural requirement to be "macho," are more afraid of losing face than women are.

However, it's unquestionably true that a VAP that might just be annoying coming from a stranger can be agonizingly painful when its source is your "significant other." And the situation is made even more complicated by the fact that couples know far more about one another than others do—which means that they know exactly what chunk of bait is likely to hurt the most. To see how this works, let's look at a very typical cross-gender altercation that relies heavily on VAPs. Assume that the couple are Tom and Mary . . .

TOM: "If you REALLY loved me, YOU wouldn't throw MONEY away like you do!"

MARY: "What do you MEAN, I *throw money away*? I do NOT!"

TOM: "Oh, YEAH? Well, what about that dress you came home with yesterday? EVEN a woman like YOU doesn't need fifty DRESSes!"

MARY: "I do NOT have fifty dresses! That's riDICulous!"

TOM: "You don't even KNOW how many you have—you ought to go COUNT them and find OUT!"

MARY: "Tom, EVen a man like YOU, with no business sense at ALL, should be able to understand that I can't go to work looking like a CLEANing woman!"

TOM: "SOME people would think you were an elitist SNOB if they heard you make a crack like THAT, m'dear!"

MARY: "I am NOT an elitist snob! How can you SAY a thing like that about me? Don't you even CARE how much you HURT ME?"

TOM: "I didn't say it, Mary, I said <u>some</u> people <u>might</u> say it! You could at least TRY to be rational!"

MARY: "Oh, so now I'm not RAtional!"

TOM: "Right. If you were RAtional, you'd know that money doesn't grow on TREES!"

MARY: "Oh, is THAT so? Well, if YOU had the guts to go out and get a decent JOB you might find out where it DOES grow!"

Because Tom knows Mary so intimately, he knows that she worries about whether she spends too much money on the wardrobe she believes her job as a real estate broker demands. He knows that a chunk of bait aimed straight at that concern will always get her going. Mary, from the same sort of intimate knowledge base, knows that Tom's major insecurity comes from the fact that she makes more money than he does—she knows that this is a weak spot she can jab at and be certain of an emotional reaction. Tom knows Mary is uneasy about how her clients would react if they knew she was married to an auto mechanic—and he knows she's ashamed of that feeling. Mary knows that Tom feels he ought to move to a career with a higher earning potential but is scared to make the move—and she knows he's ashamed of that feeling. Each of them is an expert in what will attract the most attention and provoke the strongest emotional reaction in the other. And unless they find better ways to handle their disagreements, they're going to spend their life together wading around hip-deep in a swamp of polluted language. The most tragic thing about this is that it's so easily avoided.

Now let's go back to the scenario that opened this chapter and consider how the disagreement it portrays could have been made less hostile.

ANOTHER LOOK AT SCENARIO F

Scenario F shows a situation in which negative messages can only be avoided if people decide to *lie* to one another. There are two sets of negative messages to be considered.

First: Carl and Louise do want their kids to understand that they are strongly opposed to the job change and the move; if they are honest, they will have to get that message across. Cheryl and Sam disagree with their elders' claim that they must maintain the status quo, and honesty requires them to make that clear.

Second: The two couples disagree about the idea that one spouse should be prepared to give up a job and follow the other to a new position if that would be a move upward financially and both are willing. Carl and Louise believe that applies only to wives; Cheryl and Sam see it as applying to either member of the marriage. This is really a disagreement not about the surface issue but about a principle:

Cheryl and Sam believe that men and women are entitled to equal opportunities, while Carl and Louise believe that the man's opportunities must be placed ahead of the woman's.

The first disagreement has to be dealt with immediately; there's no acceptable way to avoid it. If the second one isn't dealt with it will persist over time and is sure to come up again in future arguments. If these four people had to share a single house, or spend every Sunday together, it might be necessary to take it up and come to some sort of negotiated agreement about it, including "We agree to disagree." However, because with Cheryl and Sam moving they're going to see each other only occasionally in the future, it can safely be set aside for now.

Let's begin at the point where Cheryl has said "I don't think you understand" and explained that she'll be making a lot more money in the new job, and Sam has demonstrated his approval by saying that the move is "a terrific opportunity." Suppose Carl and Louise are familiar with the hazards of the verbal attack patterns and the benefits of refraining from their use . . .

CARL: "We do understand. We understand that you and Sam are determined to make this move, and that we can't stop you. But we want *you* to understand that we are very much against it and that—no matter how much more money is involved—we think it's a mistake."

If either parent opens the discussion this way instead of with the tirade from Carl in the original scenario, there has been no attack— just an honest statement of a position. From this opening it should be possible for the two couples to discuss the issue and come to an understanding, even if (as is probable) they continue to disagree.

Alternatively, suppose Carl delivers the entire speech about Cheryl's selfishness and her refusal to produce grandchildren, plus the claim that she's going to ruin Sam's career and the announcement that he and Louise are going to prevent that. In the scenario, everyone involved takes this multiple bait and goes to total combat stance, and three battlefield moves follow:

1. Sam responds with a "You could at least TRY . . ." VAP.

2. Louise goes into the fray with two more VAPs aimed at Cheryl: "If you really LOVED Sam" and "Even a woman like YOU . . ."

3. Carl responds to Sam's VAP with "If YOU had the brains you were BORN with . . ." in an attack on his son's intelligence and masculinity.

It is this pileup of toxic language that pushes Cheryl over the edge and sets the stage for the final confrontation that might be almost impossible to forgive and forget. It's a lot of provocation; it's natural that she should react as she did. *But she needs to remember that Carl and Louise are not talking rationally, but out of fear and hurt and their perception that she is endangering their son.* She has the opportunity to remember this and to make a move to salvage matters. She should ignore all the bait that's flying around, go to Computer Mode, and say something that is appropriate but entirely noncontroversial. The more innocuous it is, the better; the goal is to say something that *nobody* present could possibly disagree with, no matter how angry and out of control they may be. Any of these would serve . . .

- "When families have to face separation, it's hard for everybody involved."

- "Knowing that a family is going to be separated is hard for everybody involved."

- "People who love each other are always going to find it hard to face being apart."

Because this group is in the heat of battle, one such utterance probably won't be enough. Carl or Louise are likely to come back at it with, "If you beLIEVE that, how can you POSSibly go ON with this horrible IDEA?" or something similar. *Each and every such attack should then be met with another neutral abstraction in Computer Mode until the level of hostility decreases enough to make Leveling possible.* When that point has been reached, either Cheryl or Sam can say something like this:

> "I wish we could agree that this change is a good thing; perhaps someday we'll be able to. I know we can't do it right now. I also know that we all love one another far too much to let it turn into a wall that would stand between us."

Handling disagreement in this way is linguistically easy; the difficulty is not in controlling the language but in controlling the emotions.

9

REDUCING TENSION, INCREASING RAPPORT

Scenario G

"Oh, what a shame—you've already changed!" the nurse said. "You should have waited until I could bring you your hospital gown, Mr. Henderson."

John Henderson grinned at her. "It's okay," he said. "I'd rather have my own stuff on anyway."

"I'm sorry," Helen Clay said, shaking her head, "you can't do that."

"I can't do that? What do you mean—why not?"

"Look, you <u>have</u> to wear a hospital gown. That's the rule."

There was a brief silence, and then John spoke up; his voice was still pleasant, but quite firm.

"I'm not going to put that thing on," he told her. "I feel stupid with my tail end hanging out in the breeze."

Nurse Clay sighed, and clasped her hands in front of her.

"I see," she said. "We're going to be difficult, are we?"

"Oh come on, nurse—I am <u>not</u> being difficult!"

"If you weren't being difficult, Mr. Henderson, I'd see you there in that bed wearing your hospital gown, like all the <u>other</u> patients."

"I'm sorry you feel that way, nurse," he said, his face set and grim. "But I'm not going to be pushed around and packed into one of your dumb little nighties, so you can just forGET it!"

"MISter Henderson!" snapped the nurse. "<u>Please</u>! You can see how busy I am—I don't have time for this nonsense. Why don't we try to look at this in a more grownup manner?"

"You are NOT the Queen of ENGland!" John said between his teeth. "And I am NOT a CHILD, dammit!"

She gave him one cold look and said, "If you weren't ACTing like a child, it wouldn't be necessary to TREAT you like one!"

That did it. John sat straight up in bed and smacked the bedtable hard with his fist. "YOU can't lean on me like that!" he bellowed. "Who do you think you ARE, anyway? You can just go get your supervisor and send HIM down here—I have a few things to SAY to HIM!"

Nurse Clay sniffed. She laid the hospital gown down ostentatiously at the foot of his bed and gave it a few strokes, as if it were a pet.

"I had to leave anyway," she told John, looking him right in the eye. "I have to go call the doctor and let her know that you're hysterical."

And then she turned her back and swept out of the room.

"Well, while you're AT it," John shouted at her retreating back, "you can ALso tell her that I'm checking OUT of this so-called hospital!"

WHAT'S GOING ON HERE?

What's going on here is a raw struggle for power between two people who are determined to put the other down no matter what the cost. Their disagreement is very simple: The patient is determined that he will be the boss and the nurse is equally determined that *she* will be. If that means uproar and turmoil instead of the calm that a healing environment requires, so be it—they're both willing to go along with that.

POINTS OF VIEW

John Henderson is looking at the world right now through a lens of terror; he's facing major surgery and he's scared stiff. It seems to him that it's bad enough for him to have to miss a month of work and be sliced open like a watermelon, and go through all the misery that entails, without some woman he never saw before in his life ordering him around like a baby. And he knows he's going to have to deal with Nurse Clay again many times before he can go home again. As he perceives the situation, it's critical for him to establish from the very beginning—while he still has his full strength—that she can't tell him what to do.

The hospital gown isn't really the problem; the truth is, John doesn't care what he wears or how he looks. But he sees this issue as the opening move in a month-long contest, and he is determined not to lose. *I may be* <u>sick</u>, he tells himself, *but I'm not helpless, and they better keep that in* <u>mind</u>!

*****

Helen Clay has been a nurse for more than twenty years; she's seen it all. And the way she sees *this* situation is very simple: John Henderson, like a lot of middle class adult males, thinks he can come into her hospital and throw his weight around and demand special privileges—and he's *wrong*. She knows from long experience that if she lets him get the upper hand now he'll be a flaming pain in the neck for the rest of his stay.

The hospital gown isn't really the problem. The truth is, nobody would care if the man wears his own pajamas until they come to take him to the OR, and when they bring him back *he* won't care anymore about what he has on. But the way she sees it, her job is to establish from the very beginning that the hospital has rules and that he has to follow them just like any other patient.

*****

This disagreement is a classic. The question at issue—whether the patient will wear the hospital gown or not—doesn't matter to either person involved. The issues that really *do* matter, which are literally matters of life and death, ought to be the focus of attention for both patient and nurse. Yet both are so locked into the idea that one must be The Winner and the other must be The Loser that they're willing to set everything else aside and devote their energies to coming out on top in that struggle. This isn't just poor medical care—it's lunacy. And yet this scenario, or something like this scenario, happens every single day in our allegedly enlightened and sophisticated society. We will sacrifice health, education, safety, our marriages, almost *any-thing*, on the altar of the DISAGREEMENT IS COMBAT metaphor.

Both of these people are at fault. The nurse is a skilled profes-sional. She knows that much of John's bluster is due to the severe stress and anxiety he's experiencing. She knows that adding to that stress is bad for him in every way and that it's her responsibility to *reduce* the stress level so that he can go into surgery in the best possible emotional state. On the other hand, John is an adult who's determined to insist that he's in charge of his own health care and capable of making his own decisions about it—and *he also* knows that stress won't help him go through the operation and recovery successfully.

There are a number of things these two people can and should do to improve the situation. We're going to discuss three of them in this chapter—using three-part messages, using Sensory Modes, and arranging dominance displays—and then we'll come back to the scenario and see how they could be used to revise it toward a more positive outcome.

USING THREE-PART MESSAGES

Most adults in our society have a knee-jerk negative reaction to commands and criticism—to being told what to do. Every such speech act carries with it a metamessage that says "*I have the right to tell you that something about you or your behavior should be changed, and I have the right to ask you to make that change.*" Often the negative reaction isn't to the content of the command or criticism—which may be something the person really has no objection to, the way John Henderson has no real objection to wearing a hospital gown. The negative reaction is to the *metamessage*. Its effect in language interactions is threefold: It increases the level of tension, reduces the rapport between speaker and listener, and makes hostility much more likely.

There's a traditional two-part language pattern used in many forms of counseling and therapy called the "I-message," as in "I feel angry when you don't call to tell me you'll be late." Dr. Thomas Gordon has modified that pattern and improved it greatly by adding one more part. The result is the most effective strategy we have available for getting past the automatic "You can't tell ME what to do!" response and its counterproductive effects. I referred to it briefly on pages 54–56, where I recommended it as a useful form of *self*-talk. We're now ready to turn to its use in speaking to other people, which is a bit more complicated. It looks like this:

"When you (x), I feel (y), because (z)."
  1   2   3

In a perfect three-part message, each of the three empty slots is filled with an item that is concrete and verifiable in the real world. In part 1 that item is the specific chunk of behavior the speaker wants changed. In part 2, it's the emotion the speaker has toward the behavior. In part 3, it's the real-world consequence of the behavior that justifies the speaker's request for the change. For example . . .

- "When you don't turn in your sales figures by 9:30, I feel annoyed, because I can't start my reports without those figures."

- "When you bring the car home with an empty gas tank, I feel angry, because I have to go get gas before I can drive to work the next day and it's hard to find a station open that early."

The pattern should be used *exactly* as shown; there are good reasons for its every feature. Putting the "when" clause first focuses attention squarely on the listener's *behavior* rather than on the speaker's feelings, which is the best strategy. Saying "I feel angry" rather than "you make me angry" is a good strategy—if someone else has the power to make you feel a specific emotion, you would be wise to keep that information to yourself. The only change that I feel can safely be made is a switch to total or partial Computer Mode in two specific situations: when dealing with people that you know are extremely touchy and defensive, such as teenagers; and/or when you're delivering the message on someone else's behalf. For example . . .

- "When you play your stereo at top volume at night, people feel angry, because they can't sleep and they have to get up early and go to work the next day."

- "When stereos are played at top volume at night, people feel angry, because they can't sleep and they have to get up early and go to work the next day."

- "When you take files home with you for the weekend, the other sales reps feel angry, because they don't have access to the information in the files."

Notice that none of these examples contains anything that a rational person would consider a subjective opinion or a moral judgment. Each mentions just one item to be changed, and does so without any extra emotional baggage. To see why they are more likely to be heard and acted on than their badly structured counterparts, you only have to compare them with a typical complaint and criticism like this one:

156

- "When you act like you're some kind of supreme RULer around here and everybody else is just DIRT, it makes me so mad I could just SCREAM, and I'm not going to put UP with your dis-GUSTing ATtitude any LONGer!"

It's important—as always—to remember that any sequence of words set to a hostile tune is hostile language. It makes no difference how carefully you word what you say—if your goal is to construct a three-part message and use it to reduce tension and increase rapport, thereby reducing hostility, it has to be spoken neutrally. Consider the first example, on page 156:

- "When you don't turn in your sales figures by 9:30, I feel annoyed, because I can't start my reports without those figures."

You could take those same words and turn them into hostile language by saying them like this:

- "When YOU don't turn in your SALES figures by 9:30, I feel anNOYED, because I can't start my rePORTS without those FIGures!"

The second version is just one more chunk of hostile speech, and it's no more likely to get past the automatic resistance of listeners than some insult that you might choose at random.

Whenever you know that you're going to have to go into a situation where hostility is likely, and where you'll find it necessary to deliver a command or criticism, sit down ahead of time and work out a three-part message for that purpose, so that you can look at it carefully and be sure that it's properly put together. The more times you do that, the more likely it is that you'll get it right when you have to do it with no advance warning and no time to prepare.

USING THE SENSORY MODES

One of the ways that we human beings express a perception of potential rapport with another person is by saying "I think we speak the same language." That means "I believe that you perceive the world essentially as I perceive it, so that even if we don't always agree we can still work together." If I were to start writing this book in French or Cherokee you wouldn't go on reading and you certainly wouldn't feel any rapport with me.

A reliable language behavior characteristic when people are communicating under stress is that they tend to become locked into one of the set of language patterns called the Sensory Modes. We recognize these modes—automatically—by the presence of vocabulary associated with our sensory systems. For example, you would immediately be able to identify the sentence "I like the way it looks" as Sight Mode, "It sounds terrific to me" as Hearing Mode, and "I like the way it feels" as Touch Mode. You don't have to study to do this; it's part of your flawless internal grammar.

By the time we're about five or six years old we have discovered that one of the sensory systems works better for us than the others do. Some of us understand and remember better when we have information to *look* at; some get better results by listening; and then there are people who deal with the world most effectively if they can do things hands-on. Each of the sensory systems has words and phrases that make up its own vocabulary. When we're relaxed and at ease, we use them all, switching among them without hesitation or effort. But when we are worried or tense or upset—for example, when we are involved in a disagreement—we temporarily lose that easy skill and often find ourselves suddenly relying on the vocabulary of our dominant sense. In that situation, another person who speaks to us in that *same* vocabulary seems to us to be "speaking our language"; this decreases tension and increases the potential for rapport.

Suppose a boss calls in three employees—one sight dominant, one hearing dominant, and one touch dominant—and lays out his plan for a new project that will involve them all. Suppose all three employees think the plan is terrible. Because the boss has the power to hire and fire, reward and punish, this is unquestionably a situation of stress and tension. We could then expect the employees' responses to be like these three:

Sight-Dominant Mario:

"Well, I see what you mean—but it looks to me like there might be a few minor problems."

Hearing-Dominant Amy:

"Well, I hear what you're saying—but it sounds to me like there might be a few minor problems."

Touch-Dominant Jack:

"Well, I get what you mean—but I feel like there might be a few minor problems."

The more tense the speaker is, the tighter the vocabulary bind will be and the more damage a Sensory Mode *clash* can cause. In a real crisis, such a mismatch is like my suddenly switching to Cherokee in this book for readers whose language is English. It's on a much smaller scale, but the principle is exactly the same.

You can use this simple technique whenever you need to reach the goals of reducing tension and increasing rapport. Remember that you will recognize the Sensory Mode you hear if you're paying attention. You then have two rules to follow:

Rule One:

Match the Sensory Mode coming at you.

Rule Two:

If you can't match the mode, try to use no sensory language at all.

If someone who is obviously upset asks you "How bad does it look?," answer with "I don't see it as anything serious" or "It looks to me like it's pretty serious." That's Sensory Mode matching. It builds trust; it helps the other person relax a little. *Don't* answer with "I don't feel like it's anything serious" or "I feel like it's pretty serious." Both of those sequences are Touch Mode; that's Sensory Mode *mismatch*, and you want to avoid it whenever you can. If you can't think of a matching response that you're comfortable with, avoid all sensory vocabulary and just say "I don't think it's anything serious" or "I think it's pretty serious" instead. That's not as good as matching the mode, but a neutral alternative is much better than mismatch and clash.

Be careful not to underestimate the usefulness of this technique just because it's so simple. Don't be misled by the common impression of "No pain, no gain." You will be amazed at how effective this very basic communication strategy is; be glad that there's something this good that is also this easy!

ARRANGING DOMINANCE DISPLAYS

Human beings are primates. Like all primates, they like to mark out their turf and establish its limits, and they always want to know what the pecking order is in any situation. These ancient habits are so deeply ingrained that many people feel obligated to do something to demonstrate their rank and power even when there's no *reason* to do it, almost always with hostility and hostile language as a result. When the apes do these demonstrations, called *dominance displays*, they pound their chests and shriek; most human beings are a little more subtle than that.

You can take advantage of these facts when you interact with others by deliberately providing them with good opportunities for dominance displays. They'll feel better after taking advantage of those opportunities; you will have sacrificed nothing at all; and a great deal of tension-creating (and resource-wasting) jockeying for position will be avoided.

Suppose that you are a member of a committee and you've been asked to prepare and present a proposed agenda for the coming year. The other committee members will usually feel that they have to do something to demonstrate that they're your equals; the committee chairperson is even more likely to feel obligated to demonstrate that he or she outranks you. If you leave these turf-marking behaviors to chance, your colleagues may very well attack something in your agenda that really matters, and that can lead to a disagreement and confrontation.

To avoid that outcome, provide them with chances for dominance displays that you have some degree of control over. Salt your material with slightly "defective" items designed to attract your colleagues' eyes. Include figures that are just a little off, words that are incorrectly spelled, an occasional grammar error; in a list of proposed items, include one for which you can be sure that a demand for its deletion is certain. With luck, the members of the committee will be so comfortable after having demanded *those* changes—

followed by your gracious, but not too hasty, agreement—that they won't feel any need to go farther. And if they miss any of your strategic errors, you can correct those yourself on the spot or later, as circumstances require.

The last thing you need to worry about is that this will hurt your image, making you look uninformed or careless, or anything of that kind. On the contrary. As long as the items you choose are trivial rather than crucial, it will make you look cooperative and pleasant and rational and charmingly modest. Remember that your goal is not to prove your perfection but to get your material approved, accepted, and so on. Few things provoke more hostility in a group—even a group of only two—than the presence of someone who never makes a mistake.

You may have read or been told that the nonstandard dialects of English are always a handicap in the workplace. I disagree. I have always been able to rely on my own nonstandard native dialect—Ozark English—for an abundant supply of dominance-display attractors. As long as I put in enough Ozark English words and phrases for others to cluck over and convert to more hifalutin ones, the rest of my work is ordinarily left intact. The more certain I am that a particular idea is likely to cause disagreement, the more careful I am to give that idea a shape trimmed with Ozark "flaws" for those who review and edit it to repair. This doesn't make me look incompetent, it makes me look human.

I strongly recommend this strategy to you. Use it with care and restraint so that it doesn't become obvious. The only reason *not* to do it, given its positive effects, is that old compulsion to be sure you are always and without exception The Winner. I'm confident that by now you will have set that habit aside.

HE SAYS/SHE SAYS

A vast amount of the high tension and low trust in our society today is due to the recent changes in relationships between the two genders. Before roughly 1960, no matter how much lip service was given to equality of the sexes, it was understood by everyone that men were dominant and women were subordinate, especially in public life. Even a woman who truly had power—usually because she had inherited some man's large fortune—had to live with the knowledge that most men who appeared to be taking orders from her perceived *themselves*, rightly or wrongly, as only humoring her. In that context men and women knew what to say to one another, and they followed well-worn scripts.

At some point in the sixties this situation began to change dramatically. If there had been a complete reversal, if the cultural consensus were now that women are dominant and men subordinate, the communication problems would have been temporary; we could have just switched roles in the scripts. But that didn't happen, nor has any secure solution been reached. What we have today is a society in which both men and women take both roles and neither one is quite sure how to handle the situation, with resulting communication breakdowns.

The problem is not that we have Male English and Female English, but that we have Dominant English and Dominated English, with no firm attachment of either to a particular gender.

We now have a world where a woman may manage twenty male subordinates all day at the office and then go home at night to a home and family where the husband is without question the head of the household. Similarly, a man may take orders from a woman executive all day and then go home to a house where it's taken for granted that he will assume the dominant role. We demand of men that they be strong and silent, while at the same time urging them to learn to share their feelings and encourage intimacy. We demand of women that they be tender and nurturing, while at the same time expecting them to be no-nonsense take-charge superiors when that's what we find convenient. Men still rely primarily on the rules of LIFE IS A FOOTBALL GAME while pretending (and perhaps believing) that they've changed; women still rely primarily on the rules of LIFE IS A TRADITIONAL SCHOOLROOM, with the same dilemmas of belief and unawareness. This goes on even as their relative rankings change dramatically on the continuum of power. And through all of it, men and women have to try to shift back and forth between Dominant and Dominated English without awkwardness!

Not surprisingly, this is a terrible mess, perhaps most of all because it's not stable. The boundaries and limits keep shifting back and forth, driven by politics, fashion, religion, the media, and our own confusion. All we can do is wait this out, work to achieve stability, and try not to lose our nerve. We should do our best to be aware of the true source of the difficulty and to set aside the seductive myth that men and women speak different languages or dialects. *The difference is not in gender but in power.* And because we're primates, we are uneasy—and often hostile—when we're not sure precisely what today's pecking order is and dare not assume that it will stay the same until tomorrow.

If there is one basic principle that we can hold on to in the effort to decrease tension and increase trust and rapport, it is this: We train men to be far more afraid of losing face than women are expected to be. A man forced into a corner verbally is therefore more likely than a woman is to do something foolish out of panic, especially if there would be witnesses to his loss of face. Until the sands of gender perceptions shift in ways that lessen this difference, many communication moves need to be chosen with it in mind.

ANOTHER LOOK AT SCENARIO G

In this scenario the two participants make almost every communication error they *could* make short of hitting each other with clubs and stones. The nurse gives the patient direct orders and severe criticism, with nothing sheltered in presuppositions. The patient does precisely the same thing to the nurse. They both indulge in Blaming, plus sarcasm, cutesipation, and open ridicule. The nurse torments the patient with her "Imperial We"; the patient bellows at the nurse and pounds on the table. It could scarcely be worse.

Any change for the better, at any point, would affect every utterance that follows, and for every such change there would have to be a complete revision of the rest of the scenario. We don't have room for that here. In the interests of economy of space, therefore, let's look at just a few selected changes and their probable effects at that particular point in the narrative.

1. When John told the nurse that he'd rather wear his own nightclothes, she announced that he couldn't do that, brought up the hospital rule, and said "You <u>have</u> to wear a hospital gown." The result was predictably bad. Let's rewrite that exchange . . .

PATIENT: "I'd rather have my own stuff on anyway."

NURSE: "Mr. Henderson, when other patients see that someone else has been allowed to wear his own nightclothes, they feel abused, because they know that's against the rules. I know that you understand how much bad feeling that can cause."

PATIENT: "Oh ... I guess that makes sense. Okay—I'll put on the hospital gown. I <u>object</u>, mind you, but I'll do it."

NURSE: "Thank you; I appreciate your cooperation."

Here Nurse Clay has carefully avoided direct command or criticism and has used a three-part message in Computer Mode to state both the rule and one consequence of its violation. And then she has used the presupposition of "know"—that what is said to be known is *true*—to tell him she's counting on his cooperation. Notice also that when this *works* she resists the temptation to rub his nose in it and make him lose face. She does *not* say, for example, "Oh, we're going to change our <u>mind</u>, are we?"

2. If you look carefully at the vocabulary Nurse Clay and the patient use throughout the scenario, you'll discover that she relies on Sight Mode, while his language is mostly Touch Mode. This breeds tension and mistrust; it works *against* rapport. It's made worse by the fact that our culture is strongly biased *against* touch and tends to perceive touch dominant speakers as crude, or worse. Either of the two people involved could improve matters by switching vocabulary to match the other's preferred Sensory Mode.

Since the nurse is the skilled professional here, it's reasonable to expect *her* to be the one who takes that step; we'll assume that that's what happens. But remember that the option is also available to the patient. He can't be sure that the nurse is familiar with the Sensory Modes; they're not part of the standard nursing (or medical school) curriculum.

PATIENT: "I'm not going to put that thing on. I feel stupid with my tail end hanging out in the breeze."

NURSE: "This is all rubbing you the wrong way, isn't it?"

PATIENT: "Yeah—it's rough."

NURSE: "What can I do to help, Mr. Henderson?"

PATIENT: "You can get off my back and let me wear my own pajamas. Okay?"

NURSE: "Okay, I can handle that. I'm sure you know they'll put you in a hospital gown when you go to the OR, though."

PATIENT: "That's different; I understand that. No problem."

NURSE: "That's settled, then."

Here Nurse Clay has dropped the vocabulary of sight and switched to Touch Mode, to make it easier for her patient to trust her and talk to her. She has also given in on the question of the gown—which we know doesn't really matter to her. And she has not leaped to the conclusion that his touch dominant speech indicates ill will, bad manners, or a lack of respect. (For example, she has not taken "get off my back," said with neutral intonation, as an insult.)

Suppose, however, that the hospital rule is so stringent that she can't do this and she *must* insist that John Henderson go along with it. Then the exchange might go like this:

PATIENT: "I'm not going to put that thing on. I feel stupid with my tail end hanging out in the breeze."

NURSE: "It's hard for adults to have to put up with somebody laying down laws about what they wear to bed."

PATIENT: "Yeah—it's rough."

NURSE: "If there was a way to set that rule aside, I'd do it. Unfortunately, patients are stuck with it, and so are the nurses—and *everybody* feels the way you do about it. What can I do to make it easier for you to handle, Mr. Henderson?"

PATIENT: (Long sigh) "Like you said—I guess we're both stuck with it. I guess it's not such a big deal. I'll put on the blasted gown."

NURSE: "Thank you, Mr. Henderson."

3. The nurse can tell very quickly from her patient's behavior that he feels obliged to do a dominance display. She can help him out by giving him an immediate opportunity to do that. This was a part of her strategy in example #1 above—where she let him *agree* to obey the rule instead of trying to force him to—and in #2, where she asks (in both variations) what she might do to help. Here's another way she could proceed . . .

PATIENT: "I'd rather have my own stuff on anyway."

NURSE: "I know you would."

PATIENT: "I feel stupid with my tail end hanging out in the breeze."

NURSE: "Right. Everybody does."

PATIENT: "So—do I have to change?"

NURSE: "Well, let's go over it for a minute. You know you don't want to risk carrying germs from home into the OR with your pajamas—you'll want to put on a gown for that, right?"

PATIENT: "Yeah, I understand that."

NURSE: "It's up to you, then. Would you rather stay in your own stuff tonight and change early tomorrow morning, or just go ahead and change now?"

PATIENT: "I guess it's no big deal . . . I'll just go ahead and get it over with now."

If what he wore had really mattered to John, he would have made the other choice and waited till morning to put on the hospital gown. And that would have been all right, too. In either case, the nurse's metamessage goes like this: *It's true that you have to wear the gown no later than tomorrow morning, no matter how much you hate that—but notice that I am telling you so in a respectful manner.* She has switched to Touch Mode, which is the professional thing to do in talking with a touch-dominant patient. And she has provided him with a face-saving opportunity for a dominance display by offering what is called "an illusion of choice." Like asking an employee who has to go somewhere he doesn't want to go, "While you're there, would you rather stay at the Hilton or the Ramada?," this allows John Henderson to maintain his image of himself as an adult who is competent to make adult decisions.

None of the changes discussed above requires any major effort from the nurse or the patient; none requires either one to toady to the other or sacrifice any principles. What they *do*, however, is very important in a world where time is money and a serene mind is a potent tool for healing: *They make it possible for these two people to avoid a lengthy and irrelevant power struggle that is the antithesis of rational adult behavior.*

10

CONCLUSION

We have all seen the television documentaries in which people are shown washing their food and dishes and cooking utensils in filthy river water. Sometimes we know they do this because their education has been so inadequate that they're not aware that it's an invitation to disease and death. Sometimes they *do* know, and they turn toward the camera and say, "It's the only water there is—what else can we do?" In both cases, it tugs at our hearts to see their misfortune. We think how awful it must be to have to live either with such a lack of critical information or with such a lack of acceptable choices. If there's anything we can do to help, we try—but much of the time, all we can do is try not to think about it.

One of the hats I wear is the Science Fiction Writer hat. In science fiction one of our staples is the scenario in which a more technologically advanced civilization lands upon planet Earth and proceeds to turn our lives upside down, for better or for worse. If I put my SF hat on it's easy for me to imagine the horror such beings would feel as they watched our language behavior. It would strike them as unimaginably "primitive."

Here we are, scrupulously careful to keep tainted food and polluted water and toxic chemicals away from ourselves and from our families. But our language interactions—our ways of talking to one another? They are so dangerous to our health and safety and well-being that we might just as *well* be wading around up to our hips in

169

muddy rivers with our cattle, filling containers with water for drinking and cooking.

The extraterrestrials would watch with horror . . .

FIRST ET: "Good grief—how can they do that?"

SECOND ET: "Honey, think about it—they probably just don't know any better."

FIRST ET: "Surely that's not possible; don't they learn about toxic language in school?"

SECOND ET: "Remember where we are, dear—this is <u>Earth</u>."

FIRST ET: "But that's <u>terrible</u>!"

SECOND ET: "I know. Try not to think about it."

FIRST ET: "Darling, that's just not good enough—<u>we</u> have to find a way to <u>help</u>!"

Fortunately, we don't have to wait for beings from outer space to fly in and save us. The evidence about the potential our language has to harm us or help us is now readily available; some of it has been presented in this book, and the bibliography will direct you to much more. The evidence that we do have a choice—that we have abundant alternatives to harmful language—has now been set out for you. The only thing we need, in order to put this information to use in our lives, is the will to do it. It's not easy to give up old habits and old myths; it takes effort and discipline. But we are fully capable of accomplishing it.

It's time for us to climb up out of the muddy rivers; it's time to clean up our language environment and make it wholesome; and it's time to reap the benefits that will result. Reading this book was a first step; I wish you the best of luck for the rest of the way.

REFERENCES
& BIBLIOGRAPHY

ARTICLES

Addington, D. W. "The Relationship of Selected Vocal Characteristics to Personality Perception." *Speech Monographs* 35 (1968): 492–503.

A. F. G. "Notes: Judges' Nonverbal Behavior in Jury Trials: A Threat to Judicial Impartiality." *Virginia Law Review* 61 (1975): 1266–98.

Albert, M. "Universal Grammar." *Z Magazine*, December 1988, pp. 99–104.

Alter, J. "Toxic Speech." *Newsweek*, May 8, 1995, pp. 44–6.

Anderson, E. "The Code of the Streets." *Atlantic Monthly*, May 1994, pp. 81–94.

Arbeiter, J. S. "Helping Battered Patients." *OBG Management*, April 1991, pp. 25–34.

Beattie, G. W. "The Regulation of Speaker-Turns in Face-to-Face Conversation: Some Implications for Conversation in Sound-Only Communication Channels." *Semiotica* 34 (1981): 55–70.

———. "Interruption in Conversational Interaction, and Its Relation to the Sex and Status of the Interactants." *Linguistics* 19 (1981): 15–35.

Beckman, H. B., and R. M. Frankel. "The Effect of Physician Behavior on the Collection of Data." *Annals of Internal Medicine*, November 1984, pp. 692–6.

Bell, C. "Family Violence." *Journal of the American Medical Association*, September 19, 1986, pp. 1501–2.

Blakeslee, S. "Cynicism and Mistrust Tied to Early Death." *New York Times*, January 17, 1989.

Blanck, P. D. "Off the Record: Nonverbal Communication in the Court-room." *Stanford Lawyer*, Spring 1987, pp. 18–23, and 39.

————. "What Empirical Research Tells Us: Studying Judges' and Juries' Behavior." *The American University Law Review* 40 (1991): 775–804.

————. "The Appearance of Justice: Judges' Verbal and Nonverbal Behavior in Criminal Jury Trials." *Stanford Law Review*, November 1985, pp. 89–163.

Bolinger, D. "Contrastive Accent and Contrastive Stress." *Language* 37 (1961): pp. 83–96.

Cassileth, B. R., et al. "Psychosocial Correlates of Survival in Advanced Malignant Disease." *New England Journal of Medicine*, June 13, 1985, pp. 1551–5.

Catholic Conference of Bishops. "When I Call For Help: A Pastoral Response to Domestic Violence Against Women." Document released 1992.

Chambliss, L., MD. "All in the Family." *EMS Magazine*, April 1994, pp. 35–43.

Check, W. E. "Homicide, Suicide, Other Violence Gain Increasing Medical Attention." *Journal of the American Medical Association*, August 9, 1985, pp. 721–30.

Cosmides, L. "Invariance in the Acoustic Expression of Emotion During Speech." *Journal of Experimental Psychology*, December 1983, pp. 864–81.

Dershowitz, A. M. "Shouting 'Fire!' " *Atlantic Monthly*, January 1989, pp. 72–4.

Dimsdale, J. E. "A Perspective on Type A Behavior and Coronary Disease." *New England Journal of Medicine*, January 14, 1988, pp. 110–2.

Easton, N. J. "It's Cool to be Cruel: Forget the Niceties, America is on a Mean Streak." *The Dallas Morning News*, July 4, 1993.

Edelsky, C. "Who's Got the Floor?" *Language in Society* 10 (1981): 383–421.

Ehrenreich, B. "The Politics of Talking in Couples." *MS Magazine*, May 1981, pp. 46, 48.

Epstein, S. E., et al. "Myocardial Ischemia—Silent or Symptomatic." *New England Journal of Medicine*, April 21, 1988, pp. 1038–43.

Ervin-Tripp, S., et al. "Language and Power in the Family." In C. Kramerae et al., eds. *Language and Power*, Beverly Hills: Sage Publications, 1984, pp. 116–35.

Feiner, B. (Interview with Candace West.) "Communication Breakdowns: Are Your Patients Turned Off?" *Options*, August 1986, pp. 33–6.

Fellman, B. "Talk: The Not-So-Silent Killer." *Science 85*, December 1985, pp. 70–1.

———. "A Conversation with Ira Progoff." *Medical Self-Care*, July-August 1978, pp. 11–2.

Finkbeiner, A. "The Puzzle of Child Abuse." *Science Illustrated*, June-July 1987, pp. 14–9.

Fox, B. H. "Depression Symptoms and Cancer." *Journal of the American Medical Association*, September 1, 1989, p. 1231.

Friedman, M. "Type A Behavior and Mortality From Coronary Heart Disease." *New England Journal of Medicine*, July 14, 1988. p. 114. (See also other letters under same title, through p. 117.)

Gibbs, N. "The EQ Factor." *Time Magazine*, October 2, 1995, pp. 60–8.

Gold, P. W., et al. "Clinical and Biochemical Manifestations of Depression: Relation to Neurobiology of Stress." (In two parts.) *New England Journal of Medicine*, August 11, 1988, pp. 348–51; *New England Journal of Medicine*, August 18, 1988, pp. 413–20.

Goldberg, J. "Anatomy of a Scientific Discovery." *Science Illustrated*, January-February 1989, pp. 5–12.

Goleman, D. "Studies Point To Power Of Nonverbal Signals." *New York Times*, April 8, 1986.

———. "Research Affirms Power of Positive Thinking." *New York Times*, February 3, 1987.

———. "The Mind Over the Body." *New York Times Magazine*, September 27, 1987, pp. 36–9 and 59–60.

———. "Researchers Find That Optimism Helps the Body's Defense System." *New York Times*, April 20, 1989.

———. "Researchers Trace Empathy's Roots to Infancy." *New York Times*, April 28, 1989.

———. "A Feel-Good Theory: A Smile Affects Mood." *New York Times*, July 18, 1989.

———. "Sensing Silent Cues Emerges As Key Skill." *New York Times*, October 10, 1989.

Goodman, E. "The Destructive Power of Words." *Memphis Commercial Appeal*, December 27, 1995.

Gorman, C. "Can't Afford to Get Sick." *Time Magazine*, August 21, 1989, p. 43.

Granat, D. "Mother Knows Best." *The Washingtonian*, November 1992, pp. 41–5.

Gray, F., et al. "Little Brother Is Changing You." *Psychology Today*, March 1974, pp. 42–6.

Growald, E. R., and A. Luks. "The Immunity of Samaritans: Beyond Self." *American Health*, March 1988, pp. 51–3.

Guittard, C. "The Failure of Competitive Discussion and Argument." *Texas Lawyer*, December 13, 1993, pp. 18–9.

Hall, E. "Giving Away Psychology in the 80's: George Miller Interviewed by Elizabeth Hall." *Psychology Today*, January 1980, pp. 38–50 and 97–8.

Hall, S. S. "A Molecular Code Links Emotions, Mind and Health." *Smithsonian Magazine*, June 1989, pp. 62–71.

Hamill, P. "End Game." *Esquire Magazine*, December 1994, pp. 85–92.

Harris, T. G. "Heart and Soul." *Psychology Today*, January-February 1989, pp. 50–2.

Harvey, J. B. "The Abilene Paradox: The Management of Agreement." *Organizational Dynamics*, Summer 1974, pp. 1–18.

Higgins, L. C. "Hostility Theory Rekindles Debate over Type A Behavior." *Medical World News*, February 27, 1989, p. 21.

Hollien, M. "Vocal Indicators of Psychological Stress." *Annals of the New York Academy of Science* 347 (1980): pp. 47–72.

House, J. S., et al. "Social Relationships and Health." *Science*, July 29, 1988, pp. 540–44.

Hunt, A. R. "Verbal Violence Begets Physical Violence." *Wall Street Journal*, November 9, 1995.

Jones, E. E. "Interpreting Interpersonal Behavior: The Effects of Expectancies." *Science*, October 3, 1986, pp. 41–6.

Kamiya, G. "The Cancer Personality." *Hippocrates*, November-December 1989, pp. 92–3.

Kobasa, S. O. "Test for Hardiness: How Much Stress Can You Survive?" *American Health*, September 1984, p. 64.

Koop, C. E., and G. D. Lundley. "Violence in America: A Public Health Emergency." *Journal of the American Medical Association*, June 10, 1992, pp. 3075–76. (And see entire issue, a special issue on this topic.)

Kramer, M. "Time to Stop Shouting." *Time Magazine*, May 1, 1995, p. 66.

Liles, G. "Physicians Confront Violence in America." *MD Magazine*, May 1994, pp. 18–24.

Lynch, J. J. "Listen and Live." *American Health*, April 1985, pp. 39–43.

———. "Interpersonal Aspects of Blood Pressure Control." *Journal of Nervous and Mental Diseases* 170 (1982): 143–53.

———. "The Broken Heart: The Psychobiology of Human Communication." In R. Ornstein and C. Swencious, eds., *The Healing Brain: A Scientific Reader*, 1990, pp. 75–87.

Mann, C. C. "War of Words Continues in Violence Research." *Science*, March 11, 1994, p. 1375.

Mencher, B. S. "Civility: A Casualty of Modern Litigation?" *The Washington Lawyer*, September/October 1993, pp. 19–21 and 52–5.

Milstead, J. "Verbal Battering." *BBW Magazine*, August 1985, pp. 34–5, 61, 68.

Miron, M. S., and T. A. Pasquale. "Psycholinguistic Analysis of Coercive Communication." *Journal of Psycholinguistic Research* 7 (1985): 95–120.

"News Update." *Law & Order*, July 1933, p. 5.

Novak, M. "Of War and Justice." *Forbes Magazine*, March 4, 1991, p. 58.

Olsen, E., et al. "Beyond Positive Thinking." *Success*, December 1988, pp. 31–8.

Oppenheim, G. "How To Defuse a Hostile Patient." *Medical Economics*, September 5, 1988, pp. 125–34.

Phillips, P. "Domestic Violence On The Increase." *Cortlandt Forum*, November 1992, pp. 48DD–48EE.

Prothrow-Stith, D. "The Power of Nonviolence." *Best of Technology Review*, Spring 1995, p. 37.

Rauch, J. "The Humanitarian Threat to Free Inquiry." *Reason*, April 1993, pp. 20–4.

———. "In Defense of Prejudice: Why Incendiary Speech Must Be Protected." *Harpers Magazine*, May 1995, pp. 37–42.

Reibstein, L. "Up Against the Wall." *Newsweek*, September 4, 1995, pp. 24–5.

Ridley, M. and B. S. Low. "Can Selfishness Save the Environment?" *Atlantic Monthly*, September 1993, pp. 78–86.

Rosenberg, M. L. "Let's Be Clear: Violence Is a Public Health Problem." *Journal of the American Medical Association*, June 10, 1992, pp. 3071–72.

Rozanski, A., et al. "Mental Stress and the Induction of Silent Myocardial Ischemia in Patients with Coronary Artery Disease." *New England Journal of Medicine*, April 21, 1986, pp. 1005–12.

Sacks, H., et al. "A Simplest Systematics for the Organization of Turntaking for Conversation." *Language* 50 (1974): pp. 696–735.

Safire, W. "Caught Under a Blizzard of Lies." *Oakland Tribune*, January 10, 1996.

———. "Safire: Round 2." *Oakland Tribune*, January 11, 1996.

Scherwitz, L., et al. "Self-Involvement and the Risk Factors for Coronary Heart Disease." *Advances*, Winter 1985, pp. 6–18.

Seligman, J., et al. "The Wounds of Words: When Verbal Abuse Is as Scary as Physical Abuse." *Newsweek*, October 12, 1992, pp. 90–2.

———. "Emotional Child Abuse: Discipline's Fine Line." *Newsweek*, October 3, 1988, pp. 48–50.

Shea, M. J. "Mental Stress and the Heart." *Cardiovascular Reviews & Reports*, April 1988, pp. 51–8.

Smolowe, J. "An Officer, Not a Gentleman." *Time Magazine*, July 13, 1995.

Stepp, L. S. "Fighting Words." *The Washington Post*, April 25, 1994.

Toufexis, A. "Seeking the Roots of Violence." *Time Magazine*, April 19, 1993, pp. 52–3.

Troemel-Ploetz, S. "Review Essay: Selling the Apolitical." (Review of Tannen, 1990.) *Discourse & Society*, October 1991, pp. 489–502.

Walinsky, A. "The Crisis of Public Order." *Atlantic Monthly*, July 1995, pp. 39–54.

Weiner, E. J. "A Knowledge Representation Approach to Understanding Metaphors." *Computational Linguistics* 10 (1984): 1–14.

West, C. and A. Garcia. "Conversational Shift Work: A Study of Topical Transitions Between Women and Men." *Social Problems* 35 (1988): 551–75.

Williams, R. B. "Curing Type A: The Trusting Heart." *Psychology Today*, January/February 1989, pp. 36–42.

Wright, H. N. "Toxic Talk." *Christian Parenting Today*, July/August 1991, pp. 24–30.

Yankelovich, D. and J. Gurin. "The New American Dream." *American Health*, March 1989, pp. 63–7.

Zajonc, R. B. "Emotion and Facial Efference: A Theory Reclaimed." *Science*, April 5, 1985, pp. 15–20.

Zal, H. M. "The Psychiatric Aspects of Myocardial Infarction." *Cardiovascular Reviews & Reports*, February 1987, pp. 33–7.

Zimmerman, J. "Does Emotional State Affect Disease?" *MD Magazine*, April 1986, p. 30 and pp. 41–3.

Zonderman, A. B., et al. "Depression as a Risk for Cancer Morbidity and Mortality in a Nationally Representative Sample." *JAMA*, September 1, 1989, pp. 1191–5.

BOOKS

Abbott, F., ed. *Boyhood, Growing Up Male: A Multicultural Anthology.* Freedom, CA: Crossing Press, 1993.

Ader, R., ed. *Psychoneuroimmunology.* New York: Academic Press, 1981.

Ammerman, R. T., and M. Hersen, eds. *Assessment of Family Violence: A Clinical and Legal Sourcebook.* New York: John Wiley & Sons, 1992.

————. *Treatment of Family Violence: A Sourcebook.* New York: John Wiley & Sons, 1990.

Antonovsky, A. *Health, Stress, and Coping.* San Francisco: Jossey-Bass, 1979.

Argyle, M. *Bodily Communication.* London: Methuen, 1975.

Beattie, G. *Talk: An Analysis of Speech and Non-verbal Behaviour in Conversation.* Milton Keynes, England: Open University Press, 1983.

Benson, H., and W. Proctor. *Beyond the Relaxation Response.* New York: Times Books, 1984.

Blumenthal, M. D., et al. *More About Justifying Violence: Methodological Studies.* Northvale, NJ: Jason Aronson, 1988.

Bolton, R. *People Skills: How to Assert Yourself, Listen to Others and Resolve Conflicts.* Englewood Cliffs, NJ: Prentice-Hall, 1979.

Chesney, M. and R. H. Rosenman, eds. *Anger and Hostility in Cardiovascular and Behavioral Disorders.* Washington, DC: Hemisphere Corporation, 1985.

Elgin, S. H. *The Gentle Art of Verbal Self-Defense.* New York: Barnes & Noble, 1985. (Originally published by Prentice-Hall, 1980.)

————. *More on the Gentle Art of Verbal Self-Defense.* New York: Prentice-Hall, 1983.

————. *The Last Word On the Gentle Art of Verbal Self-Defense.* New York: Barnes & Noble, 1996. (Originally published by Prentice-Hall, 1987.)

————. *Success With the Gentle Art of Verbal Self-Defense.* Englewood Cliffs, NJ: Prentice-Hall, 1989.

————. *Mastering the Gentle Art of Verbal Self-Defense.* Englewood Cliffs, NJ: Prentice-Hall, 1989. (Audio program.)

————. *Staying Well with the Gentle Art of Verbal Self-Defense.* New York: MJF Publications, 1996. (Originally published by Prentice-Hall 1991.)

————. *The Gentle Art of Written Self-Defense Letters Book.* Englewood Cliffs, NJ: Prentice-Hall, 1993.

————. *Genderspeak: Men, Women, and the Gentle Art of Verbal Self-Defense.* New York: John Wiley & Sons, 1994.

————. *You Can't SAY That To Me! Ending the Pain of Verbal Abuse: An Eight-Step Program.* New York: John Wiley & Sons, 1995.

————. *The Gentle Art of Communicating With Kids.* New York: John Wiley & Sons, 1996.

Fisher, S., and A. D. Todd. *The Social Organization of Doctor–Patient Communication.* Washington DC: Center for Applied Linguistics, 1983.

Friedman, M., and D. Ulmer. *Treating Type A Behavior and Your Heart.* New York: Alfred A. Knopf, 1984.

Friedman, M., and R. H. Rosenman. *Type A Behavior and Your Heart.* New York: Alfred A. Knopf, 1974.

Goleman, D. *Emotional Intelligence*. New York: Bantam, 1995.

Goleman, D., and J. Gurin, eds. *Mind*Body Medicine*. Yonkers, NY: Consumer Reports Books, 1993.

Gordon, T. *Leader Effectiveness Training: L. E. T.* New York: Wyden Books, 1977.

Grossman, D. *On Killing: The Psychological Cost of Learning to Kill in War and Society*. New York: Little, Brown, 1995.

Justice, B. *Who Gets Sick? Thinking and Health*. Houston, TX: Peak Press, 1987.

King, S. *Danse Macabre*. New York: Everest House, 1981.

Lakoff, G. *Women, Fire, and Dangerous Things: What Categories Reveal about the Mind*. Chicago: University of Chicago Press, 1987.

Lakoff, G., and M. Johnson. *Metaphors We Live By*. Chicago: University of Chicago Press, 1980.

Lakoff, R. *Talking Power: The Politics of Language in Our Lives*. New York: Basic Books, 1990.

Lazarus, R. S., and S. Folkman. *Stress, Appraisal, and Coping*. New York: Springer, 1984.

Leech, G. *Principles of Pragmatics*. London: Longman, 1983.

Levy, S. M. *Behavior and Cancer*. San Francisco: Jossey-Bass, 1985.

Locke, S., et al., eds. *Foundations of Psychoneuroimmunology*. New York: Aldine Publishing, 1985.

Locke, S., and D. Colligan. *The Healer Within: The New Medicine of Mind and Body*. New York: New American Library/Mentor, 1987.

Lynch, J. J. *The Broken Heart: The Medical Consequences of Loneliness*. New York: Basic Books, 1977.

———. *The Language of the Heart: The Body's Response to Human Dialogue*. New York: Basic Books, 1985.

O'Barr, W. M. *Linguistic Evidence: Language, Power, and Strategy in the Courtroom.* New York: Academic Press, 1982.

Ornstein, R., and C. Swencious. *The Healing Brain: A Scientific Reader.* New York: Guilford Press, 1990.

Ornstein, R., and D. Sobel. *The Healing Brain: Breakthrough Discoveries About How the Brain Keeps Us Healthy.* New York: Simon & Schuster, 1987.

Renkema, J. *Discourse Studies: An Introductory Textbook.* Philadelphia, PA: John Benjamins, 1993.

Rothwell, J. D. *Telling It Like It Isn't.* Englewood Cliffs, NJ: Prentice-Hall, 1982.

Satir, V. *Conjoint Family Therapy.* Palo Alto, CA: Science & Behavior Books, 1964.

————. *Peoplemaking.* Palo Alto, CA: Science & Behavior Books, 1972.

Sattel, J. W. *Men, Inexpressiveness, and Power.* Rowley, MA: Newbury House, 1983.

Spence, G. *How to Argue and Win Every Time.* New York: St. Martin's Press, 1995.

Tannen, D. *You Just Don't Understand: Women and Men in Conversation.* New York: William Morrow, 1990.

Thorne, B., and N. Henley, eds. *Language and Sex, Difference and Dominance.* Rowley, MA: Newbury House, 1975.

Thorne B., et al., eds. *Language, Gender and Society.* Rowley, MA: Newbury House, 1983.

Todd, A. D. *Intimate Adversaries: Cultural Conflict Between Doctors and Women Patients.* Philadelphia, PA: University of Pennsylvania Press, 1989.

Van Dijk, T. A., ed. *Handbook of Discourse Analysis.* London: Academic Press, 1985.

Watzlawick, P., et al. *Pragmatics of Human Communication: A Study of Interactional Patterns, Pathologies, and Paradoxes.* New York: W. W. Norton, 1967.

INDEX